One Championship Season
The Story of the 1944 St. Louis Browns

Carson Van Lindt

Marabou P~~bli~~

1~

T0204475

The author wishes to thank the invaluable research assistance of Tom Boyd and Eric Van Lindt. Many thanks to Robert F. Bluthardt of The Society of American Baseball Research and Bud Kane of the St. Louis Browns Historical Society for their enthusiasm in supplying me with helpful information. Many more thanks to Arthur Richman (New York Yankees V.P. and diehard Browns fan) for always leaving his phone line open to my calls.

The great photos were made possible through the invaluable assistance of the staff at the National Baseball Hall of Fame and Museum, Inc., Jocelyn Clapp of the Bettmann Archives; and Kristen Hammerstrom of the Missouri Historical Society.

Published by
Marabou Publishing
P.O. Box 1682, New York, N.Y. 10013-1682

Library of Congress Catalog Card Number: 93-079620
ISBN: 0-9632595-6-3

Manufactured in the United States of America

This book is lovingly dedicated
to my uncle, Fred Van Lindt,
who through his tutelage
showed me what a great game this was.

TABLE OF CONTENTS

INTRODUCTION

For those who only know of the St. Louis Browns casually, one armed Pete Gray (1945) and midget Eddie Gaedel (1951) were and always will be the symbols of that organization. During their history, the Browns lost over a thousand more games than they won (3416-4465) and finished in the second division forty times, truly a frustrating record of futility.

But for Browns fans, the 1944 season produced one glorious league pennant. While the forty-two year wait for a pennant had been a long one, consider that it has taken the Chicago Cubs (forty-nine years and counting) longer with the Cleveland Indians (forty years and counting) a close second.

Still, the Browns 1944 success in all its excitement is dismissed as a fluke because it occurred during the war years (1942-'45). Many fans consider the baseball played during the war years to be an inferior game, dominated by rejects, bush leaguers, and has-beens. While it is true that more than 500 major leaguers served in the military in some capacity during those years, including many stars, the game was still played by professionals who played their hearts out. Their job was made tougher because they were forced to use below par equipment and bats that were made of lower quality wood. Travel restrictions also kept the players on the road longer.

If, as some say, the quality of play during the war years can be dismissed as inferior then so could each expansion season. With only four hundred players donning a major league uniform during the 1944 season, each team's minor league outfits contained players who were very capable of playing on the major league level.

It is true the game was missing the likes of Joe DiMaggio, Ted Williams, Bob Feller, and Hank Greenberg but the war years also gave the public just as many new stars as it had lost. Gil Hodges, George Kell, Marty Marion, Stan Musial, Hal Newhouser, Andy Pafko, Pee Wee Reese, Allie Reynolds, Snuffy Stirnweiss, Vern Stephens, and Early Wynn either made their first appearance or developed through the war years.

What many fail to note is that the St. Louis Browns organization, under the guidance of Donald Barnes and Bill DeWitt, had slowly built a winning club. Their stroke of genius came in landing Luke Sewell for the job as manager. Sewell took over the job in early '41 when the team was already out of the race and he instilled in them a winning attitude. They played .500 ball the rest of the way.

Even baseball's elder statesman, Connie Mack, noticed the progress the Browns were making and predicted that they were the team to watch as the 1942 season got underway.

In 1942 when most of the star players were still in the game and in 1945 when many of the stars returned to the game, the Browns finished in third place. History shows that the Browns fell into the second division, never to escape it from 1946 until their departure from St. Louis in 1953, but their fall wasn't because the rest of the league's stars returned home. They lost because Barnes cashed in his chips and new owner Richard Muckerman held a fire sale, undoing the gains of the Barnes' regime in order to rebuild Sportsman's Park. The team brought up youngsters not quite ready for the big leagues and traded their stars for players of lesser quality and cash.

In 1944, the Browns had to make do with what they had like every other team in both leagues. The fact that they had thirteen players classified 4-F going into the 1944 season did not guarantee them a pennant. The Indians and Athletics both had twelve players classified as such and they finished in a tie for fifth. The New York Giants of the National League had sixteen on their roster and they finished in fifth place.

There are other historical or memorable achievements made by players during the war years and none of them are as scrutinized as the Browns' pennant.

Did anyone try to diminish Tommy Holmes' 37-game hitting streak (a record until Pete Rose broke it with 44 in 1978) during the war year of 1945? Does anyone try to diminish the Cardinals three consecutive pennants and their 411 wins (.667 winning percentage) during the war years? Does anyone try to diminish Hal Newhouser's 62 wins (one-third of his lifetime total) or Dizzy Trout's 65 wins (a little more than one-third of his lifetime total) earned during the war years? Are Newhouser's Most Valuable Player Awards for 1944 and '45 tarnished? Does anyone dismiss the Tigers pennant of 1945 though they won one less game than the Browns did the year before?

The answer to all of these is no. The 1944 St. Louis Browns took part in one of the greatest pennant chases and deserve the same respect any pennant-winning team gets.

CHAPTER 1

In The Beginning

"There will be no other team in St. Louis when we get there."

> — American League
> president Ban Johnson

The American League St. Louis Browns were born from the rubble of a charter member of the American League, the 1901 Milwaukee Brewers. As members of the Western League (later to become the American League), the Brewers were a strong franchise, both financially and on the field.

Connie Mack, who joined Milwaukee in 1897, was so happy with club's progress that he bought a quarter share of the team. His experiences with Milwaukee molded him into a baseball "genius." He managed the team on the field and off, conducting all business aspects of the operation. On the road he booked the train reservations and paid and collected bills.

He guided the team to a fourth-place finish in '97 and a third place finish in '98 before dropping to sixth in '99. With the coming of the twentieth century Western League president Ban Johnson changed the name of his brainchild to the American League, giving it greater national recognition. Mack then guided the 1900 Brewers to a second place finish before leaving, by recommendation of Johnson, to take over ownership of the Philadelphia franchise.

The new league was bitterly competing with the older National League - from the players they were signing to the territory they were invading. By the end of 1900 the American League had declared itself excluded from the National Agreement which was written in 1857 to sanction rules and preserve amateur status. This action created a relatively free market in players' services, a decision which ironically worked against Milwaukee because they lost stars like Rube Waddell and Dave Fultz and replaced them with mediocre players. The other American League teams were busy signing National League stars, causing Milwaukee to suffer through their worst season in years in the American League's first year as a major league.

In 1901 under new manager Hugh Duffy, the Brewers finished 48-89, 35½ games behind the pennant-winning Chicago White Sox. Only first baseman John Anderson (8 HR, 99 RBI, .330 AVG.) was productive offensively and the best pitcher was Bill Reidy (15-18. 4.22 ERA).

The Brewers had held their first major league spring training in St. Louis in 1901, igniting rumors that Milwaukee would be moving to the Missouri city. Precedent existed for such a move; in 1878 a team called the Milwaukee Grays had moved to St. Louis.

But Milwaukee's franchise seemed safe, at first, as Ban Johnson was constantly visiting Cleveland Indians owner J.F. Kilfoyl, encouraging him to move the Indians to St. Louis. Kilfoyl didn't object to the proposition; in fact, he welcomed it if he could get three top players from the St. Louis National League team. But midway through its inaugural season, Johnson announced that St. Louis would be a member of the American League in 1902 and it would be the Milwaukee franchise which would move. For the third time in the short history of organized baseball, Milwaukee had a taste of major league status only to have it taken from them. They had brief stays in the Union Association (1884) and American Association (1891).

Brewers' owners Matt & Henry Killilea had told Johnson before the season that if they didn't get fan support in Milwaukee they would consider moving the team. But as the season progressed and the team lost games and fans, they were still reluctant to move. The brothers had all their financial interests in the city of Milwaukee and wanted assurances that they could make money in St. Louis. Actually the high salaries they were paying their players were what was killing them.

Johnson would spend a three-hour meeting telling the Killilea's about the old St. Louis Browns of the American Association and how during the 1880's they won four championships before hundreds of thousands of fans. Johnson made two more points: St. Louis was the second largest city to allow baseball on Sundays, and the sale of beer was legal.

Johnson was successful in convincing Matt, the elder Killilea, and minority shareholder Fred Gross but little brother Henry Killilea, who held controlling interest, decided to sell his interests. He wanted out of the baseball business and tried to convince Matt to sell his interest as well. Just one year later though, Henry bought into the Boston Red Sox.

With the deal to switch the franchise from Milwaukee to St. Louis consummated, the team name was changed from Brewers to Browns so as to harken back to the glory years of St. Louis baseball.

ONE CHAMPIONSHIP SEASON

Ignoring his brother's plea, Matt Killilea's Browns set up shop in a park familiar to all St. Louis baseball fans. They had been watching baseball on the site that Sportsman's Park rested on as far back as the 1860's when it was just an empty lot. Sportsman's Park would play host to more major league baseball games than any other until its razing in May of 1966.

Before the Browns' inaugural major league season Killilea had second thoughts about owning a team in Missouri. Johnson suggested that he sell his interests to local buyers. Killilea, rather than relocate his family, sold the club to Robert Hedges of Kansas City and Cincinnati lawyers J.E. Bruce and J.G. McDiarmid. Hedges was Director of the Equitable National Bank and president of Columbia Carriage Co., who made horse carriages. In the Browns' first two seasons in the American League Hedges hired local millionaire Ralph Orthwein to serve as president of the club. From 1904 until he sold the franchise Hedges took over the reins.

In spite of their later reputation as losers, the original American League Browns were favored to win the 1902 pennant. Only six players from the dismal Milwaukee roster went to St. Louis. As was typical for new American League franchises, the Browns raided the National League and stocked their roster with the best players from the National League like the Cardinals' Jesse Burkett, Bobby Wallace, Dick Padden, Jack Harper, Willie Sudhoff, and Jack Powell. As it happened the team finished in second, a respectable five games behind Connie Mack's Philadelphia Athletics.

The team toiled between fifth and eighth place for the next few seasons until 1908 when they finished fourth, fourteen games over .500 and six-and-a-half games behind the pennant-winning Tigers. They were in the race for most of the season, and the fans flocked to the park to watch their Browns.

Hedges was thrilled by what he saw and decided to put some money into Sportsman's Park. He built the centerfield section of the park with steel and cement, the first park west of the Mississippi built as such. This increased the attendance potential to 18,000 and though the Browns never came near first place for the next few seasons, Hedges made a comfortable profit.

Though the fans were still coming to the park, Hedges was growing tired of his losers. In 1913 he went through three managers.

George Stovall (50-84) started the season at the helm, improving on the prior three seasons which had seen the Browns lose over one hundred games. After a series of incidents, including spitting tobacco juice in the eyes of the umpires, he was fired in favor of third baseman Jimmy Austin.

Austin was given the reigns on an interim basis until Hedges could find an adequate replacement. After losing six of eight games, Austin was replaced by a "boy genius." In an era when players drank and swore openly, this young man didn't swear, didn't drink, and didn't play on Sundays, endearing him to Hedges. His name was Branch Rickey.

Rickey had been a member of the Browns in 1905-06, hitting .279 before being traded to the Yankees. After one tough season in New York, Rickey realized he didn't have what it took to be a ballplayer and his career was over. He turned his attention to attending law school. To pay his tuition he coached the University of Michigan baseball team.

Hedges liked Rickey's dedication and smarts and approached the youngster about becoming the Browns' general manager so that Rickey could implement Hedges' theories of "multiple ownership." Multiple ownership was another word for the farm system. The owner even purchased a franchise in Alabama in hopes that it would eventually supply him with talent. While the idea was Hedges' brainchild, history will credit Rickey.

He signed on to manage the Browns the final eleven games and got them to finish 5-6, thus avoiding another one hundred loss season. Under his tutelage the Browns improved by fourteen games before again falling back to 63-91 in '15.

At the conclusion of the 1915 season before the "multiple ownership" plan could be executed, Hedges sold the team, netting him twelve times the amount he paid for them. The team and park were purchased by a fifty-six year old growling mass of flesh named Philip de Catesby Ball who many accuse of single-handedly destroying the future of the Browns.

Ball's buying of the Browns came about because of his friendship with Ban Johnson and the dissolving of the Federal League. The upstart league had filed an antitrust suit against the American League but before Christmas of 1915 a truce was signed and in the agreement, Charles Weeghman received the Chicago Cubs franchise and Ball, who owned the St. Louis Terriers, was given the Browns. At the same time the truce was being worked out, Cardinals owner, Schuyler Britton, had put his team on the selling block. Johnson recommended that Ball buy the Cardinals, but he chose the Browns.

Ball was an extremely stubborn owner whose major flaw was to let personalities intervene with the best interests of the team. His first altercation came with Rickey. From the start the two didn't get along. Upon buying the team and listening to sportswriters speak of the "boy genius", Ball said, "I bought the team. Not the bat boy, not the groundskeeper, and not the contract of Rickey." And when he met Rickey his first words were, "So you're the goddamned prohibitionist."

*Phil Ball (photo by Strauss Studio, St. Louis,
Missouri Historical Society, Por. B-68)*

Despite the slanderous language, Rickey tried in vain to get Ball to use the farm system idea but the stubborn owner nixed it. Rickey was then resigned to front office duties as Ball installed Fielder Jones as manager of the club.

But when Rickey decided to accept new Cardinals' owner, Sam Breadon's, offer and join the nearly bankrupt club, Ball was infuriated. He tried suing Rickey for breach of contract, but the lawsuit never made it to court. Years later fans and historians could only wonder about what might have been if Rickey had implemented the farm system with the Browns instead of the Cardinals.

Rickey didn't leave the Browns' pockets empty. He had built an excellent team with a future by the time he left. His biggest contribution to the Browns was the signing of future Hall of Famer George Sisler whom he discovered at the University of Michigan back in 1913.

The decision to rid the team of Rickey was only the first in a long line of bad decisions made by Ball. The second one dragged the Browns through the mud till the day they existed no more.

In 1920, Sam Breadon convinced Ball to let him rent Sportsman's Park. He would split the costs of operating the park. It seemed like a good move for Ball because the Browns were attracting the bulk of the city's population. Especially when they challenged for the pennant in '22. Ball netted a huge profit that year and was confident the Browns were going to have a championship within the next couple of years. He expanded Sportsman's Park to 32,000 (from 18,000).

In 1926 there was a champion in St. Louis but it was the Cardinals and quickly the allegiance of the Missouri city was shifted to the team in red socks. The Cardinals were winning and accumulating four times more in attendance than the Browns. Ball ended up subsidizing the Cardinals' operation. With the Browns getting worse with each passing year and the Cardinals getting better, he tried with no success to break the contract. With the money Breadon saved, the Cardinals put together the best farm system in baseball, the very kind that Rickey couldn't convince Ball to organize.

Ball's attitude hurt the Browns further during their losing years. In 1929 he hired spies to follow the Browns on road trips because he questioned manager Dan Howley's strategic moves. Though Howley only guided the Browns to two .500 plus seasons out of three, that was more than a lot of St. Louis Browns managers could claim.

Howley and the press caught the drift of what was going on and it became a big story. When Ball read that Howley said, "I'm the manager and not Ball," Howley was fired.

Ball's stubborness hampered the Browns chances to produce winners in spite of their talent. In 1923 he sent rookie pitcher Charlie Root to the Cubs after he failed to win a game (0-4). Root would help the Cubs win the pennant in 1929.

In 1930 when their best player, Heinie Manush, failed to show at a luncheon that Ball had arranged for friends, Manush was immediately traded to Washington for another star, Goose Goslin.

Goslin was traded when Ball heard that Goslin wanted out of the losing atmosphere in St. Louis. At one time the Senators had a superstar outfield made up of former Brownies in Goslin, Manush, & Fred Schulte.

During the "Roaring Twenties", the Browns had embarked on their best decade in terms of won-loss percentage. A fourth-place finish in '20 and a third-place finish in '21 set baseball up for one of its earliest exciting pennant finishes. The 1922 Browns were the best team they ever had that didn't win the pennant.

The '22 team was a powerhouse, leading the American League in batting, slugging, runs, triples, stolen bases, saves, earned run average, walks and strikeouts. They were the first major league team to have four players with one hundred runs batted in. And they featured one of the greatest outfields ever, if not the best. In leftfield there was Ken Williams (39 HR, 155 RBI, .332 Avg.), in centerfield there was "Baby Doll" Jacobson (9 HR, 102 RBI, .317 Avg.) and in

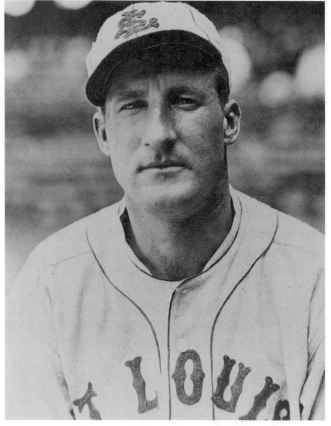

*Goose Goslin (National Baseball Library
& Archive, Cooperstown, N.Y.)*

rightfield there was Johnny Tobin (13 HR, 66 RBI, .331 Avg.).

The infield was weak on the left side but Marty McManus who hit .312 with 109 runs batted in played second base and George Sisler was at first.

Sisler, a seven year veteran, turned in his best season ever. He hit .420 (still a record), knocked in 105 runs, led the league in hits (246), triples (18), runs scored (134), and stolen bases (51) enroute to winning the Most Valuable Player Award.

Catchers Hank Severeid (.321) and Pat Collins (.307) not only excelled at the plate but behind it, handling what was probably the Browns' best ever pitching staff.

Led by Urban Shocker, who had a third consecutive twenty win season (24-17, 2.97), Emil Vangilder (19-13, 3.42), and Ray Kolp (14-4, 3.93), St. Louis battled neck and neck with the Yankees before a crucial August head-to-head series. The Yankees got the better of the series and though both teams continued to play hot ball throughout the summer, the Yankees emerged the champions by one game.

The Browns lost fourteen of twenty-two games to New York but their hopes were seriously damaged when the Yankees acquired Joe Dugan in late July from the Red Sox. The third baseman hit .286 and was flawless defensively for New York down the stretch giving them a big lift. The Browns cried foul, and Commissioner Landis took notice. He agreed the late acquisition was unfair and instituted what we know today as the June 15th trading deadline.

For the last time the Browns were picked by many as heavy favorites in 1923 but a sinus condition sidelined Sisler for the season. His big bat was sorely missed from the lineup and the pitching struggled as the Browns finished fifth.

Sisler returned in 1924 not only as the first baseman but as manager. The team climbed to fourth place but they were another year older. They managed to finish third in '25 but after two consecutive seventh place finishes and a surprising third place finish in '28 the Browns sank into the second division throughout the thirties, giving alternate meaning to the "Depression." Not even Rogers Hornsby, who was brought in to manage in 1933, could bring St. Louis' American League club out of the doldrums. In one game during

*George Sisler (National Baseball Library
& Archive, Cooperstown, N.Y.)*

that season the Browns played before a crowd of 34, not including the vendors.

Though St. Louis' junior circuit fans suffered through the hard times, they were not without great players to cheer for. There was Heinie Manush (1928-'30), Goose Goslin (1930-'32), Harlond Clift (1934-'43), Sammy West (1933-'38), Beau Bell (1935-'39) and Bobo Newsom (1934-'35, 1938-'39 and '43).

Goslin and Manush, both eventual Hall of Famers had problems with Ball and hated the losing attitudes on the team but that didn't keep them from turning in great seasons. Manush hit .378 and .355 in his two seasons before being traded for Goslin. Goslin hit .326, .328 and .299 before being traded.

Clift was one of the most popular Browns ever. He was a consistent power-hitting third baseman who went unrecognized because he played for the consistent second division Browns. From 1936-39 he led all third basemen in home runs. His thirty-four home runs in '38 was a record for third basemen until Eddie Mathews broke it in 1953. He was also a threat on the field. In 1937 he set major league records with 405 assists and 50 doubleplays plus an American League record with 637 total chances. Clift played for St. Louis until 1943.

Outfielder Sammy West was crushed when he was traded to St. Louis from Washington. The Senators were a team on the rise and would win the pennant in '33 as the young star toiled in the outfield for the eighth-place Browns. But West played hard and batted .300 in five of the six seasons he was in St. Louis.

For two seasons Beau Bell was a solid performer. In '36 he hit .344, leading the American League in hits with 218 and doubles with 51. In '37 he knocked in 117 runs while batting .340. But in '38 he only hit .262 and after beginning the following season at .219 he was traded to the Tigers where he fared no better. Alcohol speeded his demise and he was out of baseball by '42.

The Browns had a few decent pitchers during those rough seasons. George Blaeholder won ten or more games for seven consecutive seasons and is credited with inventing the slider, but is more famous for surrendering Babe Ruth's 600th home run, and Lefty Stewart won twenty games in 1930.

But none had the character of Bobo Newsom. Newsom became a member of the Browns three different times during his career. When he was drafted by the Browns from the Cubs organization, he refused to report. After being coaxed into signing with St. Louis he boldly predicted he'd win fifteen games. Skeptics, including the front office, laughed and

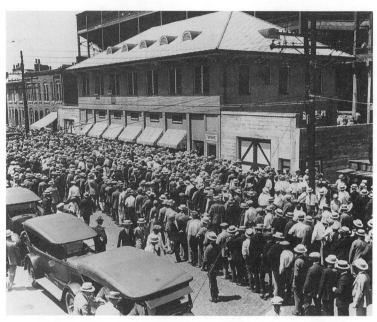

The 1922 Browns packed them into Sportsman's Park.
(National Baseball Library & Archive, Cooperstown, N.Y.)

many had a good time writing about his 9-16 start in the daily papers. But "Bobo" turned it around and finished with a 16-20 record, making good on his prediction. He got off to an 0-6 start in '35 before being shipped to Washington. In 1938 he returned to St. Louis and won twenty games. But in '39 he was traded only to return in '43. After going 1-6 with a 7.44 earned run average, management bid him adieu forever.

The cocky Newsom never had a chance to clash with Ball. The difficult owner died in 1933, leaving his estate and his percentage of the Browns (87%), to his wife and two children. Unlike Hedges, Ball's investment in the Browns was not lucrative as he lost over $300,000 during his tenure.

The running of the ballclub was left to his lawyer, Louis B. Von Weise, but only because no buyer could be found. Running the team was a miserable chore for Von Weise and it became evident in the team's continued failure. The estate had serious trouble operating the club after the 1935 season when the Browns attracted a season total of only 80,922 fans.

That miniscule gate attraction was not only the result of the team's poor play but Ball's earlier reluctance to install lights. Cardinals owner Sam Breadon was an early advocate of night baseball and pleaded with Ball to install lights after the 1931 season. Night baseball during the "Depression" could only have helped Ball financially but he saw no future in it. Von Weise stuck by Ball's decision after his passing. It wouldn't be until 1940 that Sportsman's Park hosted games under the artificially lit skies of St. Louis.

Von Weise believed Rogers Hornsby, who had been hired by Ball before his passing, was the man to bring winning days to the Browns. He gave full rein to the Hall of Famer to rebuild the team, but the Browns actually got worse.

St. Louis had become a nightmare for visiting American League teams. With attendance horribly low, visiting teams had trouble paying their hotel bills and train expenses. The Ball Estate decided it was time to sell the team but history had shown that would be no easy task. Von Weise sought the help of an old Brownie friend in Branch Rickey and at the end of the 1936 season, a hustling businessman took a shot at turning the Browns into winners.

ONE CHAMPIONSHIP SEASON

CHAPTER 2

Building A Winner

"You've been in baseball for 20 years now. You owe it to yourself to go over and listen to them."

— Cleveland Indians
owner, Alva Bradley,
speaking to Luke Sewell

Louis B. von Weise called Branch Rickey one afternoon and asked him if he wanted in on a deal. If Rickey could find von Weise a new owner, Rickey would earn a commission totalling up to $25,000. Being the money-conscious type, Rickey had no problem in accepting the proposal. Knowing that his right-hand man, Bill DeWitt, had married a woman whose best friend was the daughter of a wealthy businessman, Rickey knew he could swing a deal.

DeWitt's marriage to Margaret Holekamp made him a frequent visitor to the home of the president of the American Investment Company, a small-loan firm listed on the New York Stock Exchange. The man's name was Donald Barnes.

ONE CHAMPIONSHIP SEASON

It didn't take DeWitt long to convince Barnes that buying the Browns would be a good investment (or perhaps a good write-off). But before Barnes would enter into this proposition he had to be assured that DeWitt would join him.

DeWitt, who once served briefly as an office boy for Rickey during Ball's tenure, received Rickey's blessings and rejoined the Browns organization.

DeWitt grew up in a poor family and had to spend his summers working instead of playing with kids his age. Ironically, his first job was in baseball. He worked as a soda vendor at Robison Field, the original home of the Cardinals.

He moved up to office boy when Rickey was promoted from the field to the office. Rickey took a liking to the young DeWitt and helped guide the youngster in his studies. When Rickey left the Browns for the Cardinals, he took DeWitt with him. By 1936, DeWitt was the Cardinals' Treasurer, and Vice-President in charge of almost thirty minor league teams.

Barnes came up with the idea of getting the public to own the team. Stock in the team was offered at five dollars a share, and the public responded. About 1500 shareholders invested close to $100,000. Barnes put up $50,000 of his own money, got DeWitt to throw $25,000 into the pot, solicited several other investments, plus a loan from the American League and became the new president of the St. Louis Browns.

In November of 1936 the deal was completed, and Barnes immediately started spending the working capital wisely. Unlike his predecessors, Barnes looked to the future and hired new scouts to fill the farm system with young, promising players. The practice of selling off the future for cash - a practice that was mastered by Ball - was a thing of the past.

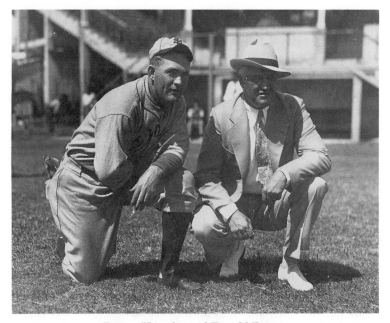

Rogers Hornsby and Donald Barnes
(Missouri Historical Society, Sports 73)

He also avoided hiring former greats for gate appeal. When he took over the club, Rogers Hornsby was manager. But after a 25-50 start in '37 and Hornsby's refusal to stop betting on horses, he was fired.

Then in '39, Barnes and DeWitt turned down Babe Ruth's pleas to manage the club, opting instead to expand their farm system by purchasing the Toledo club.

The new Browns regime made many speaking engagements around St. Louis during the winter of 1936-'37, trying to get Missourians interested in their American League sons. People took notice that Barnes and company actually cared about winning and many insiders thought the '37 season would attract a lot more fans. They were right: Though the Browns lost 108 games, attendance increased by 30,000.

ONE CHAMPIONSHIP SEASON

The team improved slightly in 1938 but in 1939 they suffered through what would be their worst season ever. The team lost one hundred and eleven games and finished *sixty-four and a half* games behind the Yankees. Horrible attendance caused Barnes and DeWitt to think about getting out of town.

In May, with the team hopelessly out of the race, the Browns looked to the future of the club. They traded their "ace," Bobo Newsom, along with Red Kress, Jim Walkup, and Beau Bell to the Tigers for pitchers Roxie Lawson, Bob Harris, George Gill, and Vern Kennedy, oufielder Chet Laabs, and infielder Mark Christman. At the time the key to the trade was the pitchers.

The Browns lost eighteen of their next twenty games. For the remainder of the '39 season Kennedy (9-17), Harris (3-12), Lawson (3-7), and Gill (1-12) contributed to the Browns worst ever team earned run average (6.01). Newsom helped the Tigers win the pennant the following season. Ownership was being attacked for making a lousy trade, but several players helped the Browns' cause.

Laabs would improve the outfield defensively (despite his sore arm which was fully taken advantage of), and his .300 batting average aided an otherwise dismal offense.

Christman would have to wait for the departure of Clift to grab hold of the third base job but he played hard for St. Louis' farm club, Toledo. He had a reputation as a fine fielder and would be called to the big club in time for the 1943 season. His break came when Clift, whose power totals were deteriorating despite his youth, was traded to Washington for Ellis Clary. Clary took two weeks before reporting to St. Louis so that he could get his family settled. Christman was given a shot at the third base job and never relinquished it.

Elden Auker lays one into Joe Kuhel of the White Sox
during a game in 1942. (Missouri Historical Society)

While the public was only conscious about their team's record at the time (attendance in '39 was 109,156), the Browns were slowly improving their ballclub and farm system. Still the frustration of playing before few fans made improvement difficult. With no money coming in, the Browns almost had to sell players that had a good future with the team.

ONE CHAMPIONSHIP SEASON

With the new decade upon them, Barnes and DeWitt spoke with American League president, William Harridge, about moving the franchise. Both talked about moving the team to Los Angeles, taking over Wrigley Field and the Pacific Coast League Los Angeles Angels club.

The other owners were neither surprised by nor opposed to the request. Everyone knew that St. Louis could not support two teams, Boston and Philadelphia were having the same problems. Even the Cardinals were toying with the idea of moving to Detroit.

Scheduling would be a problem because of the long train ride to Los Angeles. Train trips out to the west coast would also cost extra for the teams, but Barnes and DeWitt felt that Los Angeles would support the losing team. The city had been one of the top attendance draws for years in the Pacific Coast League.

Negotiations went on throughout the 1940 season and into the 1941 season. Philip Wrigley, owner of the Chicago Cubs and the Pacific Coast League Los Angeles club, had trouble deciding if he wanted to sell the park and team in Calfornia. The Browns offer of close to one million dollars stared him in the face everyday. It was already agreed that the Cardinals owner, Sam Breadon, would give the Browns $350,000 to leave town.

Meetings dragged on into December of '41. With the bombing of Pearl Harbor, the Browns chance to move to Los Angeles was scrapped.

After the '44 season, when stock in the Browns had risen, Barnes considered moving to Los Angeles again. But two years after the war was over the Browns were in such financial straits under new management that they couldn't possibly match the offers Barnes had made. Los Angeles would have to wait till the end of the next decade to see major league baseball.

Key players in the Browns future began making appearances in 1940. The team had improved twenty-four games, breaking out of the second division. That was something they hadn't done since finishing fourth in 1929. Knowledgable baseball men were noticing St. Louis' progress.

Through key acquisitions the Browns built a powerful lineup, finishing fourth in runs scored and slugging average. Walt Judnich (24 HR, 89 RBI, .303 AVG.), Harlond Clift (20 HR, 87 RBI, .273 AVG.), George McQuinn (16 HR, 84 RBI, .279 AVG.), Johnny Berardino (16 HR, 85 RBI, .258 AVG.) and Rip Radcliff (7 HR, 81 RBI, .342 AVG.) made opposing pitchers think before chucking the ball.

But with only one starter, Elden Auker (16-11, 3.95), and one reliever Bill Trotter (7-6, 3.77) having any value on the mound, the team finished a distant sixth. When Fred Haney got the team off to a 15-29 start in 1941, Barnes wasted no time in finding another manager. In early June, he contacted Luke Sewell.

Sewell was the younger brother of Joe who earned a mantle in the Hall of Fame after thirteen excellent seasons where he hit .312 and amazingly struckout only 114 times in over seven thousand at bats. His youngest brother, Tommy, made a pinch-hit appearance for the Cubs in 1927 but his career ended shortly afterwards.

Luke had spent his first five seasons in the major leagues as an apprentice under the great catcher Steve O'Neill and a two year platooning stint with Glenn Myatt. He soon developed a reputation as an excellent receiver, becoming the team's regular catcher in 1926 and holding the post until 1932. He wasn't a power hitter, relying more on spraying the ball around the park.

Luke Sewell ridded the team of losers and helped build a winner. (AP/Wide World Photos)

He was traded to the Senators in time for the 1933 season and found himself in the World Series at year's end. He collected only three hits in the series (.176) as the Giants took the series in five games. After a disappointing '34 season he was traded to the Browns, but before he could wear the uniform, he was sent to the White Sox. He played with Chicago for four seasons when he was released. The Brooklyn

Dodgers picked him up but after riding the bench for a month, he took a job as coach for the Indians.

Sewell was quite happy coaching for Cleveland. He avoided the rigors of managing when he turned down an offer to succeed Roger Peckinpaugh as manager at the conclusion of the '41 season. But a week later he got the phone call from Barnes.

His initial response was to stay away. A position with the Browns, on the field or in the office, was a demotion. When he agreed to meet Barnes, Sewell booked a return flight to Cleveland. But when Barnes promised Sewell a strong voice in the operation, he accepted the job and used his plane ticket to go home and pack his bags.

Sewell was delighted to see the advancements the organization was making. Browns' management was seriously looking to create a winner instead of settling for a couple of games improvement over the previous season. No longer were they going to sell prized players to compensate for lost revenue from empty seats. Proof came during the 1940 season when the Tigers waved $200,000 in Barnes' face for George McQuinn, Harlond Clift, and pitcher Emil (Hillbilly) Bildilli. Barnes turned them down. Sewell knew he had made the right decision and put his own plan of action into play.

The 41-year-old manager's first and only plan was to rid the team of those with losing attitudes, regardless of their play on the field. Some of those players were talented and would be good sale or trade bait.

The players responded to their new manager's wants and played .500 ball for him. The Browns had improved by only three games but it was the first time since 1920-22 that they had improved on their won-loss percentage for two consecutive seasons.

But during the winter of '41-'42 the Browns financial situation worsened. The stock that originally sold for five dollars a share was now selling at two dollars. The six minority directors refused to put any more money into the team. DeWitt was asked to take a pay cut, which he did. The Browns had to drop five farm teams and four full-time scouts, as well as their publicity director. The American League worsened things by eliminating the seven additional night games they had awarded the Browns only the year before. In 1940 the Browns had more attendance in their fourteen night games than they did in the other 63 home games combined. Apparently Commissioner Landis and the National League owners thought it was better to loan the team $25,000, overriding the American League owners' decision to schedule more night games.

Just when things were looking bleak for Barnes and it appeared the Browns might have to sell some of their best players, Richard D. Muckerman, heir to the St. Louis City Ice & Fuel Company, bought almost $300,000 worth of new stock, becoming the new Browns' vice-president. He would be a silent partner until Barnes decided to cash in his chips after the 1945 season.

Suddenly Barnes had some capital to work with. With the news that Branch Rickey was leaving the Cardinals, Barnes offered the "Mahatma" a $25,000 salary and a block of stock to run the team. Rickey's family urged him to stay in St. Louis but the Philadelphia Phillies and Brooklyn Dodgers also showed a lot of interest. No one knows where this would have left DeWitt but, luckily for him and probably because of him, Rickey took the job offered by Brooklyn. Even if the war were to close baseball as it was rumored, Rickey would still be paid his salary by the Brooklyn management. This was the security that led Rickey to the Dodgers. Again, Browns fans can only wonder what might have been. Perhaps Jackie Robinson would have worn a St. Louis Browns uniform.

As the 1942 season got underway, Sewell ridded the team of .300 hitting Roy Cullenbine, whom he considered the laziest player he had ever seen, and his doubleplay combination of Johnny Berardino (drafted) and Don Heffner. Replacing Cullenbine in the outfield was Glenn McQuillen and replacing Heffner and Berardino in the middle of the infield were newly acquired Don Gutteridge (from the Cardinals) and rookie Vern Stephens.

Stephens added pop to the shortstop position (14 HR, 92 RBI, .294 AVG.) and Gutteridge's intensity (90 runs scored and 854 chances at second) solidified the middle of the infield. McQuillen (.283) offered future promises but at the end of the season he was called into military service.

Stephens was one of the few players the Browns were able to say was their property from the sandlots to Sportsman's Park. He was signed as a seventeen-year-old for a $500 bonus. His father wanted him to stay in school but the youngster was able to convince him that he would pick up his education during the off season. His batting stance was reminiscent of Joe DiMaggio's and, at times, he played like the great one. But unlike DiMaggio, Stephens thoroughly enjoyed the nightlife and it may have been his love of it that stunted what otherwise could have been a Hall of Fame career.

For Cullenbine, Sewell got a front-line pitcher in Steve Sundra and a valuable outfielder in Mike Chartak. He was making the right moves. At the conclusion of the 1941 season, the National League champion Brooklyn Dodgers offered Dolph Camilli, Cookie Lavagetto, and cash for George McQuinn and Harlond Clift. Sewell and DeWitt wanted to make this deal badly. Camilli was a powerhouse and one of the finest fielding first basemen ever and Lavagetto was one

Vern Stephens was one of the outstanding players to emerge during the war years. (National Baseball Library & Archive, Cooperstown, N.Y.)

of those scrappy hungry players everyone loved to have on their team. Camilli was just coming off a league-leading 34 homers, 120 runs batted in season but the gods were staring down at the Browns as neither McQuinn or Clift could clear waivers. Lavagetto would voluntarily enlist in the Naval Air Force before the '42 season began and Camilli was in the service by '44. As the old saying goes, "some of the best trades are the ones that are never made."

The 1942 team started out hot then cooled off considerably by July, but they still had enough steam in them to finish the season with eighty-two wins, their most since 1928.

St. Louis' .276 batting average was the best in the league and baseball still hadn't felt the crunch of the war. Their lineup boasted Chet Laabs (27 HR, 99 RBI, .275 AVG.), Walt Judnich (17 HR, 82 RBI, .313 AVG.), George McQuinn (12 HR, 78 RBI, .262 AVG.) as well as Stephens, Gutteridge, and a slumping Harlond Clift.

The third baseman's career had slowly deteriorated. The once gifted hitter was still only 29 years old. Sewell worked hard with him, but eventually gave up midway through the 1943 season. Clift was one of the few men who was ever disappointed over being traded by the Browns.

While the lineup had some punch, Sewell's masterpiece would be the putting together of a pitching staff. His years as a catcher helped as did his coaching staff of Zack Taylor and Fred Hofmann, both former catchers. Upon taking over the team he molded the pitching staff and they lowered their earned run average in three successive seasons.

The Browns were steadily improving. The only thing that could stop them would be the war which was picking up steam. By the time the 1943 season started, war, not baseball, was on everyone's mind.

ONE CHAMPIONSHIP SEASON

CHAPTER 3

War & the "Hot House Gang"

*"With a war on, the great players gone and many
more bound to leave, the job confronting the 1944
baseball prognosticator is ten times as tough as it
was in the days of peace."*

— sportswriter
Dan Daniels

When the Japanese bombed Pearl Harbor in December
of 1941, baseball immediately understood the ramifications.
The team owners of each league played with the idea of sus-
pending the game so that the military services could use the
huge supply of young athletes. One man was dead set against
that idea. He was the President of the United States.

Five weeks after the bombing, President Franklin Delano
Roosevelt presented Commissioner Kenesaw Mountain Landis with what is known today as the "green light letter."

*I honestly feel that it would be best for the country to keep
baseball going. There will be fewer people unemployed and every-*

31

body will work longer hours and harder than ever before. And that means that they ought to have a chance for recreation and for taking their minds off their work even more than before. — FDR

To the pleasure of a majority of the nation the game would continue, but Landis stressed that baseball players should not receive any kid glove treatment in the drafting procedure. A baseball player would not be classified any different from John Q. Public.

Baseball's actual involvement in the war began ominously during a game at the Polo Grounds on May 27th of 1941. The game was halted by President Roosevelt's speech about the U.S. getting directly involved in the war. He did not declare war, but everyone knew things would be different.

By the beginning of the 1942 season, baseball had made a list of operational changes. Every club was to admit servicemen free, and the prices of cigarettes, soda, peanuts and other concessioned items were lowered. Players, managers and umpires were to receive ten percent of their earnings in War Bonds. Signs were to be placed at every vantage point within each stadium urging fans to buy war bonds and war stamps. All east coast clubs were to institute systems for handling an air raid. The list went on.

During the five seasons (1941-45) that the U.S. was at war, hundreds of benefit games were staged by major and minor league clubs to raise money for War Bonds, the USO, the Red Cross, and the Army and Navy relief funds, which aided the families of servicemen. The major leagues alone would contribute almost three million dollars to war charities.

Sixteen million men in their twenties and thirties were off to war between 1941-45. In 1941, with the United States not yet in the war, the minor leagues were being raided by the draft. One hundred and ninety-three players were drafted that year, but it hardly left a dent in the vast minor league system that operated in those days. Early in the season Hank Greenberg was the first big name player to be inducted into the service.

The need for manpower wasn't great in the early going, but with the war expanding Landis refused preferential treatment for the players and agreed they should serve the country like any other citizen. As the 1942 season got underway, teams began losing some of their best players (a total of 61 major leaguers were serving) but the game still featured most of its stars.

But as the 1943 season began, major league baseball was beginning to field many minor leaguers and formerly retired players. Over two hundred major league players were in the armed forces. The Browns lost two fine players, outfielders Glenn McQuillen and Walt Judnich.

McQuillen, a singles hitter, hit .283 in '42 after cups of coffee in '38 (.284) and '41 (.333). While Judnich was replaced by Milt Byrnes (.280 average) and Mike Chartak (10 home runs) neither was the threat Judnich was at the plate.

Judnich, in his first three seasons in the majors ('40-'42), averaged 18 homers, 85 runs batted in, and a .300 batting average. His arm was like Joe DiMaggio's and he led American League outfielders in fielding during his first three seasons.

Trading during the war years was especially frustrating. Owners had to wait and see who would be classified 4-F. Trading for any other classified player would only be a roll of the dice with the draft board.

DeWitt made a strong bid to acquire first baseman Hal Trosky of the Indians. A deal seemed near in June of '43 but

Trosky wasn't sure what he wanted to do. He had sat out a year and a half because of migraine headaches and requested that he be traded near to his home in Iowa. His choice was the Browns or White Sox but Cleveland general manager Roger Peckinpaugh did not like DeWitt's offering of Chartak or Hal Epps and sold Trosky to Chicago instead. Sewell's intention was to play Trosky in the outfield which would have made that situation even more crowded than it was. Peckinpaugh wanted Kreevich but Sewell was unwilling to part with him. Again, some of the best trades are the ones that are never made.

Kreevich was a special acquisition of Sewell's. The outfielder had been released by Connie Mack's Athletics when he couldn't control his drinking problem. He was a consistent .300 hitter his first few seasons with the Chicago White Sox before alcohol got the better of him. In 1940 he hit .265, in '41 it was down to .232, and in '42 it was .255.

He no longer had the powerful throwing arm which earned him eighteen assists in 1939, but Sewell felt Kreevich could contribute to the team and offered him $2,000 more than the outfielder requested. Sewell enlisted a friend, who eventually became one of the originators of Alcholics Anonymous, to watch over Kreevich throughout the season. Even with the addition of other wild boozers like Sig Jakucki and Tex Shirley, Kreevich reduced his intake and once again became a fine ballplayer.

By the end of the 1943 season there were serious rumors about drafting players classified 4-F, those who suffered from ailments ranging from hernias and bad backs to poor eyesight. Branch Rickey, always looking forward, suggested that teams pool their players if 4-F's were taken. Luckily for the game and the fans who watched it, that idea was cast aside. It was also a blessing for the Browns who had thirteen such players on their 1944 roster.

Mike Kreevich (AP/Wide World Photos)

With the news that 4-F's would not be touched, baseball breathed a sigh of relief. The government also decided on April 9th not to take anyone married, over the age of twenty-seven, and working in a defense plant. This kept Chet Laabs, who had passed his physical and was to report to service on April 15th, on the playing field.

The war not only determined which players were being taken, but team travel as well.

ONE CHAMPIONSHIP SEASON

Commissioner Landis and the presidents from both the American and National Leagues, William Harridge and Ford Frick, respectively, were contacted by Joseph B. Eastman, director of the Office of Defense Transportation, about cutting back on wasted mileage. He asked that road trips be reduced from the usual four trips to three. Teams played longer road and homestands and then had three or four consecutive days off, but it saved more than five million miles of railroad travel.

The travel restrictions were put in effect immediately, altering spring training. Teams were forced to train in the north which made training conditions horrendous. Snow covered the grounds of many sites, forcing players to practice indoors. The only teams excluded from northern training sites were the Browns and Cardinals who were allowed to practice in Missouri. The whole situation was easier to contend with at that time than it would have been today. Those were the days when players lived in or near the city they played for. By training in the north, players were able to stay with their war plant jobs for as long as possible.

Because of the uncertain draft status of many players, spring training was delayed for most teams. The Browns were to begin on March 10th but moved it back to the 20th.

For the second consecutive year the team held camp in Cape Girardeau, Missouri, a small town about 120 miles south of St. Louis. It was a far cry from their San Antonio, Texas training site.

Luke Sewell and half a dozen Browns, as well as about 24 minor leaguers from the Toledo Mud Hens, got off the train in Cape Girardeau in mid-March and were greeted by Mayor R.E. Beckman and about 200 fans in a driving sleet and rainstorm.

While most teams were forced to make do with whatever indoor facilities were afforded them, the Browns had the opportunity to hold spring training in the Southeast Missouri State Teachers College gymnasium, Arena Building. In walking distance was Houck Field Stadium where they were able to change in and out of their uniforms, and the Fairground Park where they played their games.

A batting cage was brought into the gym. Netting was hooked up above so that windows weren't shattered. Players were hitting, but fielding and baserunning skills were suffering. While the gym was beneficial, it wasn't an adequate replacement for a baseball diamond. The pitchers were having a hard time throwing because some 350 Naval trainees were also using the gym. The pitchers were tossing some batting practice but unable to throw at normal speed. Also hurting the team was the fact that the Arena was also being used by Toledo. The Browns were forced into working either morning sessions or afternoon sessions, never getting in a complete day's work. What looked like a head start on the rest of the league became a hinderance.

From the beginning the bad weather kept the team indoors. The playing field at Fairground Park was muddy from the constant rain and freezing temperatures. At nearby Houck Field Stadium, the team would run laps after each workout regardless of the temperature.

Aside from trying to get proper workouts going for the club, one of Sewell's chief concerns was the catching situation. During the winter the team had traded Frankie Hayes as part of Sewell's quest to rid the team of negative vibes. His .188 batting average didn't help his cause. Perhaps as punishment for his bad attitude with the club, Hayes was dealt to the Philadelphia Athletics who had finished last in seven of the past nine seasons and next to last, the other two. Nevertheless, Hayes would have an all-star season with Philadelphia in '44.

The hole at the catching position was the result of the team's worst trade in the Barnes era. Going for youth and the future, the Browns traded the popular and future Hall of Famer Rick Ferrell to Washington for catcher Angelo Giuliani. Surprisingly, Sewell allowed the trade. Ferrell was a veteran who along with the coaching staff helped mold the pitching staff.

Giuliani meanwhile was a member of the Browns organization in 1936 and appeared in sixty-six games batting a poor .217. He spent a couple of seasons with the Brooklyn Dodgers and the Washington Senators when he was aquired by St. Louis. He appeared in forty games for Washington in '43 and batted .226.

Luck shined down on the Browns again when Giuliani refused to report to St. Louis, opting to retire instead. When Barnes phoned Washington's owner, Clark Griffith, that Giuliani had to be replaced, the stubborn owner refused. Barnes took his case to the commissioner's office and Landis agreed that Giuliani had to be replaced by another player of equal value.

Sewell wanted outfielder Gene Moore. Sewell remembered that the outfielder had hit the Browns well in '43. When Moore was in Montreal (as property of the Dodgers) back in 1942, he hit 29 home runs and drove in 99 runs, but in the majors he was strictly a line drive hitter. Apparently Griffith figured his starting three outfielders were good enough and agreed to send him to St. Louis.

Despite the good fortune, Barnes, DeWitt, and Sewell still had to make a decision on their catching situation. Sewell had come out of retirement to put on the shin guards for six games back in '42 when there was a shortage of catchers, but that was only going to be a last resort for him in '44.

Twenty-four year old Joe Schultz would be given a look but he was young and had a poor throwing arm. They decided to bring up Frank Mancuso and Red Hayworth, two catchers whose brothers were much better players at the same position.

Mancuso arrived in spring training with a healed broken leg from his stint in the military. A second lieutenant in the Army, he got tangled in his parachute, hit some trees, and broke his leg. His back still bothered him, no help when it came to catching pop flies.

Hayworth had the same trouble with pop flies but not because of injury. Hayworth, despite discussions with Sewell and his coaching staff, assumed that catching a pop fly in the major leagues was no different from the minors. But the wind currents in the double decked major league parks were much different and it took a while for Hayworth to master pop-ups behind the plate. Despite those negatives both Mancuso and Hayworth were fine receivers and they played well while sharing of the position. Hayworth in particular impressed Sewell who was happy with the young man's ability to learn quickly from experience. Pitcher Jack Kramer liked working with Hayworth and that tandom seemed to work well as the season progressed.

Also worrying Sewell was Laabs' decision to stay at the war plant job in Detroit. The loss of his bat forced DeWitt to hunt for a power hitter. With few choices he chose average over power and signed Frank Demaree who had been released by the Cardinals. Demaree was 33 but hit .291 as a utility outfielder and pinch hitter. He had enjoyed his best years with the Chicago Cubs during the late thirties. He appeared in eleven World Series games with the Cubs. He didn't make a good impression with Sewell however because he showed up extremely overweight.

Players were slow getting to Cape Girardeau. As of March 22nd, only thirteen players were in camp. But with each passing day a player or two joined the crew. Within a week the whole squad was there, but because of the bad weather only two workouts had commenced outdoors.

General Manager Bill DeWitt was at camp and very pleased with the arena. But before he could get excited about the upcoming season, the players succumbed to the flu. Nelson Potter, Joe Schultz, Al Hollingsworth, Ellis Clary, and Frank Mancuso were all struck within a week severely cutting their practice time. It appeared they might miss opening day. Clary would come into the season with only two spring at bats and Potter would not even get to pitch during the spring. Rough luck even struck the coaching staff as Freddie Hofmann was struck in the face by a thrown ball during an indoor drill. A few teeth were knocked out but he was back in camp the next day.

With players and coaches falling to illness and thrown baseballs, DeWitt's patience was tested with the arrival of Mike Chartak to camp. The outfielder who DeWitt and Sewell were counting on to supply some power for the outfield came into camp 37 pounds overweight.

To be sure no one else let their weight get the best of them, Sewell would turn the thermostat on high when the team worked out in the Arena Building. Not only were players sweating off excess fat but he was preparing them for the summer heat in St. Louis. This practice led the press to nickname the team "The Hot House Gang." After practice, regardless of the temperature outside, Sewell would send his men to run one or two miles around the track at Houck Field Stadium.

*Vern Stephens, Luke Sewell & Don Gutteridge find time to fool
around during Spring Training (Missouri Historical Society)*

Chartak worked his way through the Yankees farm system, eventually getting an invitation to the big club's spring
training camp in 1939. Trying to break into an outfield of
Charlie Keller, Joe DiMaggio, and George Selkirk was an im-
possible task and despite having a good spring, he was sent
back down to Newark. He was hitting .342 when he broke
his leg. He would finally make it to the big club in '42 but
he wasn't given much of a chance. After going hitless in five
pinch hit at bats, he was traded to the Senators. Though
Chartak hit .217 for Washington, Sewell, who always liked
his bat, traded for him. His 1943 stats (10 HR, 37 RBI, .256
AVG.) suffered with his weight increase during the last half
of the season. Seeing that it carried over into the winter,

DeWitt gave him an ultimatum. Lose 37 pounds or be cut from the team.

Of the twelve pitchers that showed up to camp only six (Al LaMacchia, George Caster, Bob Muncrief, Al Hollingsworth, Steve Sundra, and Denny Galehouse) had pitched in the majors in 1943. Four (Sam Zoldak, Weldon West, Jack Kramer and Tex Shirley) had pitched in the minors and two (Sig Jakucki and Ray Campbell) had not pitched professionally at all.

Despite the inexperience, Sewell was counting on Sundra, Kramer, Potter, Muncrief, and Galehouse to do most of the starting. Unfortunately Galehouse would choose to stay at his war plant job as did Muncrief. Potter fell so ill that he couldn't pitch during the whole of spring training.

Kramer was highly touted on the merits of his minor league record but still was a question mark coming into the 1944 season. The handsome pitcher was the last to report to spring training camp because he was not getting paid what he sought. DeWitt finally gave in to his demands.

Kramer was one of those guys with enormous talent who has trouble showing it statistically. In his first three seasons with the Browns, he posted records of 9-16, 3-7 and 4-3 with no earned run average lower than 5.16. Yet in the minor leagues he had won twenty for San Antonio and in '43 went 8-1 for Toledo including throwing the first no-hitter in the American Association since 1935. Sewell and DeWitt felt he would soon come through and turned down all offers for him.

Sundra was the key man in the rotation. He was coming off an astonishing 15-11 record for the sixth place Browns, but he had already passed his military physical. Though he was 34 years old and married, the call of the military was still

Frank Mancuso & Frank Demaree (Missouri Historical Society)

imminent. The ruling that would later spare Chet Laabs from donning fatigues had yet to be announced.

Sundra was a favorite of Sewell's. Sewell wished he could multiply Sundra's attitude by twenty-five. Sundra didn't care whether he was pitching for a first place team or a last place team. He pitched with one frame of mind. To win.

The dazzling righthander began his career in 1936 when as a 26 year old rookie for the New York Yankees. He was a member of their '38 and '39 championship teams, compiling an 11-1 record with a 2.76 earned run average in the latter season. After he struggled in '40, the Yankees sent him to Washington which then traded him midway through the '42 season to the Browns. Coming to the Browns for pitcher Bill Trotter (twenty game winner in San Antonio) and .300 hitter Roy Cullenbine, he frustrated fans who thought St. Louis got the worst of the deal.

He soon changed their minds, finishing the '42 campaign with eight wins in eleven decisions. Sewell had worked with him to come up with a change of speed. His reputation as a hard thrower had everyone sitting on his fastball. After a great season with a team that struggled in '43, Sundra knew he could help the team win in '44 but he was playing on borrowed time.

The Browns beat their Toledo farm team four games to three, but they were far from impressive. The Browns had lost three of the first five games before turning it around. Though the batting cage was used a lot during their time indoors, the Browns did not fair well with the bat in the exhibition games. Starters Mark Christman (.077), Mike Kreevich (.125), Red Hayworth (.143), Don Gutteridge (.176), and George McQuinn (.214) were having a hard time meeting the ball. Sewell had his men each taking over one hundred swings following the first couple of games. Even those that were hitting (Gene Moore .500, Frank Mancuso .364 and Vern Stephens .264) were forced to endure the constant swinging. Treatment for blistered hands kept team trainer Bob Bauman busy. The extra swinging didn't show any positive effects in the remaining games of the series.

Leaving Cape Girardeau, the Browns headed to St. Louis for the City Series which was played every year before the season began. The Browns usually won the series, having taken every one since 1935.

The games were sloppy and unexciting as one game witnessed twenty-five base on balls and another twenty-five base hits. The games were played before small crowds in rainy weather. The Cardinals won the series four games to one.

Denny Galehouse, George Caster, Sam Zoldak, Bob Muncrief,
Al Hollingsworth, Jack Kramer & Nelson Potter made up part
of the Browns pitching staff. (The Bettman Archive)

DeWitt leaned back in his chair in the second floor office in Sportsman's Park after tossing the morning paper on his desk. The consensus amongst many of the baseball writers was that it would go down to the wire between the Yankees and Senators, with a strong challenge from the Tigers.

But he knew he had a good team this season. The Browns had been building a successful franchise for six seasons. Nineteen forty-three had been a setback but not bad enough to return the Browns to their historic ways.

ONE CHAMPIONSHIP SEASON

CHAPTER 4

A Record-Setting Beginning
(April 18-May 4)

"I won't predict we'll win the pennant but we may come close."

— Luke Sewell

With the magic of opening day, the stories of death and destruction that jumped at everyone from the front pages of newspapers across the country were temporarily cast aside. Owners, believing that the box office would be hurting, were pleasantly surprised to see fans flock to the stadium. In total almost 300,000 fans showed up for the four games in each league.

The Browns arrived in Detroit to no better weather than they had experienced in Cape Girardeau. Though the skies were clear the temperature struggled to get in the upper forties. Despite the chilly weather, 28,034 fans filed into Briggs Stadium to witness the beginning of the 1944 championship season.

ONE CHAMPIONSHIP SEASON

The Tigers still looked to be in good shape, especially since their lineup had hardly changed. They did lose Dick Wakefield, 1943's rookie sensation, but he would return in mid-season. Rudy York would still be patrolling first base and Doc Cramer's .300 batting average was back for another season.

The pitching staff still sported two of the best in the league in Hal Newhouser and the opening day pitcher, Dizzy Trout. Detroit did lose sixteen game winner Virgil Trucks to the military, but management was confident in youngsters Rufus Gentry and Stubby Overmire.

Going for St. Louis in the opener was Jack Kramer who took the mound in hopes of giving the Browns their eighth straight opening day victory.

Kramer and Trout battled the hitters through the cold breeze that whipped up during the game. Gripping the ball may have been hard for both pitchers, but the sting the batters felt when connecting evened things out. The Browns scored a first inning run on a groundout by McQuinn. The score remained 1-0 until the ninth inning.

Stephens, who had failed to get the ball out of the infield on his first three trips to the plate, led off the ninth inning with a shot into the leftfield stands to give the Browns an insurance run and a 2-0 lead. It turned out to be an important run because after striking out the first two batters in the bottom of the ninth and getting two strikes on Pinky Higgins, Kramer surrendered a long home run to the third baseman.

Kramer seemed rattled by the blast and gave up a single on his first pitch to Jim Outlaw. Sewell wasted no time in taking out the tired pitcher and brought in George Caster.

Caster got the Brownie bench nervous when he walked Don Ross to put the tying run on second. But the 36-year-

Left to right — Nelson Potter, Luke Sewell and Jack Kramer discuss pitching before season opener. (The Bettman Archive)

old reliever settled down and got Bob Swift to pop out, preserving the opening day victory, 2-1.

The following day Sundra battled the Tigers, only allowing one run (a home run to Rudy York) in the fourth inning. The Browns only collected seven hits but won 3-1.

On the final day of the series the bats came alive for both teams. Sig Jakucki made his first major league appearance in seven years and gave up five runs in a shaky performance.

But the Browns attacked Newhouser for five runs by the third inning and three more off two relievers to sweep the series with an 8-5 victory. It was now on to St. Louis and hopefully the eager Brownie fans.

ONE CHAMPIONSHIP SEASON

The area surrounding Sportsman's Park during the 1940's was a thriving haven of restaurants and shops. Grand Avenue, beyond the rightfield pavilion, nestled the tracks that led the streetcars to the park. The residential area in which the park was located offered fans the assorted aromas of barbeques and burning leaves from its homeowners. On days when the park was packed, homeowners would rent their garages or back yards to drivers who couldn't find a spot for their cars.

Much to the disappointment of Barnes and DeWitt, who repeatedly walked to the window of the Browns' office, the red and cream colored streetcars descending on the park were unloading only a handful of people. Many of them made their way to the Sullivan Street entrance which led to the 65¢ bleacher seats.

Under misty skies the drum and bugle corp marched across the field ahead of the waving American flag and a parade of sailors from the United States Naval Armory. Between the pitcher's mound and home plate the Coast Guard Band played enjoyable music. And in what may have been an opening day first, the Browns and White Sox lined up on the baselines for the national anthem instead of marching to the centerfield flagpole. Mayor A.P. Kaufmann threw out the first ball.

Everything on the field and around the park looked picture perfect. The huge scoreboard beyond the leftfield seats rose high in the air with ads from GEM Blades, Dizzy Dean's likeness promoting Falstaff's Baseball Broadcasts ("I broadcast 'em like I pitched 'em. Tune in Me and Johnnie"), and the War Chest sign (sponsored by Hyde Park beer), overseeing the linescores of each game around the league. Mavrakos chocolates and Alpen Brau Gold beer were advertised from the leftfield line to left-center. Below the huge screen in rightfield, Griesedieck Bros. Beer, the major league standings and a transportation ad for the streetcars and buses completed what made those parks unique from today's sterile look. And for the only time during the season the grass was a beautiful green. By June because of the constant use and the torrid summer sun, it would begin to discolor. By August there were hardly any traces of green, just patches of brown grass.

In spite of the beauty of the park, less than 4,000 fans showed up to watch the undefeated Browns begin their home season, and almost one thousand of those fans were kids and servicemen who were admitted free.

The kids, seated in the leftfield bleachers, were called the "Browns Brigade" which was the Browns' version of the Cardinals "Knothole Gang." The "Brigade" (like the knothole's) was made up of kids from the YMCA, Protestant Sunday Schools, Catholic churches, and an African-American Boys Club.

Regardless of the size of the crowd the Blake Harper hot dogs, often referred to as the best ballpark hot dogs of the time, were being devoured by kids while the Falstaff, Hyde Park, Alpen Brau, and Griesedieck Bros. Beer flowed from the taps.

The players dressed in the dim and hollow clubhouse below the stands. Some ate the sandwiches the clubhouse boy had run out to get while others either played cards or just sat by their lockers. The clubhouse with its bare concrete floors, wet from footprints that spread from the shower stalls to the lockers, was relatively cool as electric fans blew from both ends of the small chamber. The players dressed with no particular enthusiasm as they slowly made their way to the dugout.

Sewell, already gambling early in the season, went with Nelson Potter in the home opener. At the time it was a questionable move since Potter had not pitched to a batter all of spring training. Not even during a squad game.

The righthander was coming off an impressive 10-5 season with a 2.79 earned run average. Except for coming down with the flu in spring training he seemed relatively healthy. If there was any concern, it was for his knee.

Potter had torn cartilage in his right knee while on the track team in college. He was still good enough to be signed by the White Sox but when he hurt his arm adjusting his pitching style to his injured knee, the Sox dropped him. The Cardinals signed him but only stuck with him for one season. He then endured a knee operation and three seasons with the Philadelphia Athletics compiling a 19-38 record.

Potter was traded to the Red Sox in 1941 and after struggling with his control, his knee was operated on again. This time he saw a surgeon in Chicago who informed him that the last operation had resulted in the removal of the wrong cartilage. He spent the 1942 season in Louisville where he worked hard on his screwball and curveball, but it wasn't until he was traded to the Browns that he came up with a slider. Adding that pitch to his repetoire made him a valuable pitcher on Sewell's staff. Despite feeling a little weak from the flu, his knee was feeling as strong as ever.

His job was made easier when for the fourth game in a row the Browns wasted no time in getting on the board. In their half of the first Don Gutteridge started off with a single. One out later McQuinn singled Gutteridge to third followed by a walk to Stephens which loaded the bases. Frank Demaree then hit a sacrifice fly for a 1-0 lead as Mike Kreevich walked up to the plate.

Kreevich lifted a long fly ball to leftfield. Wally Moses ran back to the wall but could only look up as the "Browns

Brigade" raised their hands in unison in trying to catch the home run.

The four runs scored in the opening inning seemed plenty until the seventh inning when with the score 5-0 (after another Kreevich homer) Potter, incredibly still on the mound, was getting understandably weary and surrendered a three-run homer to Hal Trosky. He was able to regain his composure and shut the door on the rest of the White Sox for St. Louis' fourth consecutive win.

The mist that, present throughout the home opener, turned to rain the following day, cancelling the game and forcing a double header on the twenty-third.

St. Louis' pitching excellence continued when Kramer won his second game of the season. Once again he pitched a shutout until the late innings, this time losing it in the eighth inning when McQuinn's dropping of a ball thrown from Christman at third allowed the Sox new life and two runs. Kramer helped himself out with a two run homer in the second.

In the nightcap the Browns were losing 3-2 in the bottom of the eighth when they, like all good teams, took advantage of an error and pushed a couple of runs across the plate. The White Sox left town losers of three straight.

After two days off the Indians camped out in Sportsman's Park for two games. The Browns were in the strange but comfortable position of being in first place with a 6-0 record. With the Indians fielding pretty much the same team they fielded in '43 when they finished in third, Barnes and DeWitt eagerly awaited a big crowd. Their disappointment over attendance continued as only 960 paid to see the Browns' victory in the opener. About 200 more came the following evening, a game which the Browns also won.

ONE CHAMPIONSHIP SEASON

Winning their first eight games was an American League record and it brought about remembrances from Missouri old-timers. There were recollections of the old 1884 Union Association St. Louis Maroons who won their first twenty games and eventually won the pennant with a record of 94-19.

The notion that the Browns would tally that kind of record was strictly for dreamers but then again the notion that the Browns could win the first eight games in a season - let alone eight consecutive games anytime - was also reserved for dreamers.

The team boarded a train to Chicago immediately after the game. The Browns needed one win to tie the all-time record set by the 1918 New York Giants and the 1940 Brooklyn Dodgers for most consecutive victories at the start of the season. Of course the record wouldn't assure the Browns of a pennant as the Giants and Dodgers both finished in distant second in those respective seasons.

Kramer opened the series in Chicago and fell behind 1-0 in the second when Hal Trosky scored on an infield out. But Kramer didn't allow another hit until the seventh inning and no runs for the remainder of the game. Meanwhile St. Louis chipped away for single runs in the fourth, sixth, and eighth innings to record their ninth consecutive win.

Al Hollingsworth made his first appearance the following afternoon in an attempt to break the consecutive wins at the start of the season record. The thirty-six year old southpaw was staked to a three-run lead but Sewell knew that might not be enough. Hollingsworth was being hit hard, though the ball always found itself in the mitt of a Brown.

In the second inning the Sox loaded the bases with two out but Skeeter Webb struckout looking and then leading off the sixth Guy Curtwright hit a screaming liner into deep

Jack Kramer is congratulated after pitching the Browns to their ninth straight victory. (AP/Wide World Photos)

leftfield. Milt Byrnes ran and made a spectacular grab before crashing into the cement wall. Byrnes escaped injury.

But by the seventh inning Hollingsworth couldn't escape trouble. Three sharp hits and an infield out brought two runs home for Chicago and then in the eighth after there were two outs and no one on base he walked Mike Tresh. He worked the count full to Vince Castino before the rookie ripped a double that brought home the tying run.

ONE CHAMPIONSHIP SEASON

The score remained tied going into the bottom of the ninth inning with Caster now on the mound. Caster had pitched two scoreless innings of relief against Chicago the week before so Sewell was confident that Caster had the inside track on the Sox' hitters.

Webb led off the ninth with a roller to Stephens at short. In his haste to make a play Stephens took his eye off the ball and bobbled it. After Myril Hoag grounded Webb to second, Sewell ordered Caster to walk the powerful Trosky.

Curtwright then ripped the first pitch into left-center-field. Byrnes, who had already robbed Curtwright of a hit, and Epps both ran for the ball but this one was beyond the reach of both. Webb scored easily and the Browns had lost their first game of the season. The crowd of 3000 in Comiskey Park erupted in loud applause as the Sox players congratulated each other.

The immediate concern in the clubhouse after the game was not the loss, but a hand injury Mark Christman suffered in the fourth inning when bending down for a grounder. Quickly lowering his hands, he jammed his throwing hand into the ground. He did bat in the fifth and flied out but what was later diagnosed as a slight tear between the index and second fingers of his throwing hand started to swell. Indicative of the era he would only miss the next five games.

The final day of the month fell on a Sunday which meant a doubleheader. Bob Muncrief, strong from spending the winter working in a shipyard but still needing fine tuning work on his pitching because he missed spring training, was banged around for five runs in the opener but he was spared a loss when St. Louis rallied to tie the game in the eighth.

Sewell elected to go with Potter in the tenth though he had pitched nine innings only three days earlier. The choice raised eyebrows from all Browns fans who knew that the

*Mark Christman was one of the finest third basemen
of his time. (National Baseball Library
& Archive, Cooperstown, N.Y.)*

bullpen had hardly worked since the season began. Sewell
even had Bill Seinsoth and Ray Campbell sitting cold in the
"pen" but this really was Potter's spring training. Sewell
needed Potter to get as much work as possible. Potter proceeded to surrender the game winning double to Leroy
Schalk. The loss gave the Browns a modest two-game losing
streak.

ONE CHAMPIONSHIP SEASON

Their first losing streak ended a couple of hours later when with the help of a Stephens home run Tex Shirley won his first game of the year, 5-4.

The Browns returned home for a short three-game series with the Tigers before heading on an eighteen game road trip. Despite winning ten of their first twelve games the Browns still could not attract a large crowd. The total attendance for the three game series was a little more than 3000 and that included the second sub one thousand of the young season.

Sundra started the first game of the series but left the game after one inning because of soreness in his arm. Sewell didn't want to take the chance on hurting one of his best pitchers. A little rest, he hoped, would make him good as new. Injuries, especially in those trying war years, could have sunk the Browns faster than a Nazi submarine. An inning after Sundra went to the clubhouse second basemen Don Gutteridge injured his hand on a play at second. Luckily for St. Louis their sparkplug only missed four games.

Jakucki was called in to pitch and was not effective as he gave up six extra base hits in a 4-3 loss, their first to Detroit in the young season.

St. Louis downed Detroit in the final two games of the series, continuing their dominance of them, behind the pitching excellence of Kramer and Potter. The twin wins kept the Browns two and a half games up on the second place Yankees. Yet despite the 12-3 start, Sewell was not all that happy.

The record could not hide the fact that after Sundra, Kramer, and Potter the pitching staff was shaky. The team was only hitting .240 and that worried Sewell. The manager's orders upon leaving St. Louis for Cleveland was that he

Trainer Bob Bauman & Luke Sewell escort Don Gutteridge from the field after a hand injury. (The Bettman Archive)

wanted the team to report to the park early on game day for some extra batting practice and sharpening of pitching skills.

Adding to his worries was the word that Sundra would be lost for the season, not because of his sore arm but because Uncle Sam decided he was fit for service. A probable fifteen-game winner was now missing from the rotation.

The agony of losing Sundra was somewhat eased when DeWitt got in touch with pitcher Denny Galehouse. The pitcher, working in a war plant in Akron, Ohio, had decided he would not play baseball in '44, but he eventually succumbed to DeWitt's plea and agreed to report to wherever the Browns were playing on the weekends.

Galehouse in a full season was good for ten wins. The previous three seasons he flashed records of 9-10, 12-12 and 11-11 with fine earned run averages.

Thus far the pitching staff of Jack Kramer (4-0, 2.06 ERA), Nelson Potter (3-1, 1.54 ERA), Bob Muncrief (0-0, 3.37 ERA) and Sig Jakucki (1-1, 5.40 ERA) were manning the rotation with Tex Shirley (1-0, 4.77 ERA) and Al Hollingsworth (0-0, 3.37 ERA) periodically filling in.

Veteran George Caster (1-1, 1.45 ERA, 3 Saves) just fifteen games into the season, had already figured in a third of the team's decisions. Bill Seinsoth was sent back to Toledo and Ray Campbell reported for military service, neither making an appearance for St. Louis in their short stay. Seinsoth would be called up later in the season but again would sit in the bullpen. He would win sixteen games for Toledo that year.

While George McQuinn (0 HR, 5 RBI, .292 AVG.) and Vern Stephens (2 HR, 14 RBI, .315 AVG.) were doing their share with the bat, key players like Don Gutteridge (0 HR, 6 RBI, .211 AVG.), Mark Christman (0 HR, 2 RBI, .250 AVG.) and Gene Moore (0 HR, 7 RBI, .233 AVG.) were struggling.

The combined hitting of catchers Frank Mancuso and Red Hayworth (.222 with two runs batted in) kept Sewell and DeWitt searching for backstop help. As the season progressed, Hayworth would become a very smart catcher and Sewell was more apt to pencil him into the lineup everyday.

The Browns surprised a great many with their fast start. But as attendance and sportwriters throughout the country attested, there were few believers. Sewell knew the team had a long way to go. The weather was getting warmer but it wasn't long before the Browns were cooling off.

A *Record-Setting Beginning*

May 5, 1944

	WON	LOST	GB
St. Louis Browns	12	3	—
New York Yankees	7	4	3
Boston Red Sox	6	7	5
Philadelphia Athletics	5	6	5
Washington Senators	5	6	5
Cleveland Indians	6	8	5½
Chicago White Sox	5	8	6
Detroit Tigers	5	9	6½

ONE CHAMPIONSHIP SEASON

CHAPTER 5

The Same Ol' Browns!?!
(May 7 - June 11)

"We're getting our spring training done as we go along."

— Luke Sewell

The Browns opened their eighteen game road trip in Cleveland's League Park. The Indians were splitting their season between the rundown park and the newer Municipal Stadium, which until 1948 was only used on weekends or holidays.

The odd shape of League Park with a rightfield fence only 290 feet from the plate, forced managers to throw lefthanders. The fact that the fence rose forty feet in the air wasn't much help to pitchers. It forced righthanders to throw outside. Because Hollingsworth was the only lefthanded pitcher on the staff and because he had just pitched, Sewell was forced to go with righthander Bob Muncrief.

Muncrief pitched very well but got tired by the sixth inning. The problem was that St. Louis could not score a run while he was in the game. He left for a pinch hitter in the seventh with the score 2-0.

The Browns scored a run in each the seventh and eighth innings to tie the game but the Indians were not through in the bottom half of the eighth.

Jakucki, working his second inning of relief, took a deep breath before throwing his first pitch in the eighth. Roy Cullenbine, who was one for three thus far, stepped into the batter's box.

Jakucki decided to start him off with a fastball, exactly what Cullenbine was waiting for. Cleveland's rightfielder drilled the pitch over the forty foot right-field screen for what turned out to be the winning run.

The Sunday doubleheader, played in Municipal Stadium, witnessed Kramer winning his fifth game in a row, 7-4, before the Browns bowed in the nightcap, 3-2. Hollingsworth surrendered three runs in the first inning to the Indians and held them scoreless the rest of the way. Unfortunately St. Louis could not get anything going against Al Smith.

As was the practice for teams during the war years, the Browns were to make two stops before heading to Washington. Two exhibition games had been set up in Norfolk and Newport News, Virginia to face the Navy and Army teams, respectively. Sewell asked Zach Taylor to take his pitchers and catcher Red Hayworth directly to Washington so that they could get rested up before taking on the team that many predicted would be on top or near it by season's end. At this point though the Senators were three and a half games behind St. Louis.

The Senators were slow out of the gate but their won-loss record hid an important statistic. Despite winning five of their last seven games, they had lost six games in the young

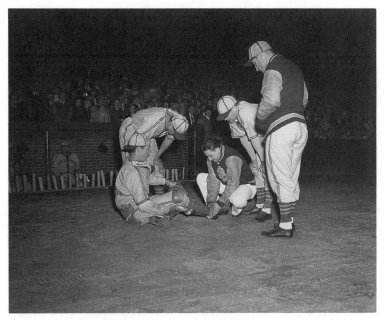

*Catcher Frank Mancuso is tended to after injuring himself in
a game against Washington. (The Bettman Archive)*

season by one run. Regardless of the tough start, almost
20,000 fans showed up at Griffith Stadium.

Knuckleballer and former Brownie Johnny Niggeling dazzled St. Louis for nine innings in a 5-1 win. The Yankees
were beating the Tigers at the same time and moved to
within half a game of the Browns.

Despite the possibility of falling out of first place, the
Browns brass was more concerned with their catching corps.

During the game, catcher Frank Mancuso ran into a box
rail while chasing a foul pop. During the evening his knee
swelled up which worried Sewell. Mancuso joined Hayworth
on the injured list and that left young Joe Schultz Jr. to do
the catching.

ONE CHAMPIONSHIP SEASON

Schultz didn't posess a good throwing arm so Kramer was busy checking baserunners instead of concentrating on the hitters. He managed to do all right until the Senators came to bat in the bottom of the eighth of a 2-2 tie. A throwing error by Schultz allowed the Senators to score what turned out to be the winning run. The Yankees had beaten the Tigers again and the Browns temporarily lost first place but the next day Mancuso limped back into the lineup by going three for three and Kreevich drove in two runs with a triple as St. Louis bats came alive to the tune of fifteen hits, breaking a three game losing streak, in a 6-4 triumph.

Although the war's dipping into the player pool had virtually given every team in the league a shot at the pennant, the Philadelphia Athletics may have been the only team exempt from that possibility. The Athletics hit a total of fifty-nine home runs in the two previous seasons combined and lost two hundred and four games in the same time span. But someone forgot to tell the Browns as they were swept in the unfriendly confines of Shibe Park.

Hollingsworth failed in his third consecutive start as Philadelphia cranked out seventeen hits against the lefthander, and relievers Jakucki, Sam Zoldak, and Lefty West.

The next afternoon the Browns were swept in a doubleheader which saw them hit into eight double plays. The rally killers ruined fine performances by Potter and Shirley who both threw shutouts through six innings. St. Louis would lose the opener 4-3 in eleven innings and 2-0 in the nightcap.

Sewell and his men caught the evening train to Boston where they would meet the struggling Red Sox. A good series would prime the team up for the Yankees who they were to visit afterwards. New York had swept the Indians to move two games up on the Browns. The Senators were only a half game behind St. Louis.

Sewell, trying to shake the Browns and their dismal .234 team batting average, benched Kreevich and Moore in favor of Zarilla and Demaree. Neither of the replacements were hitting the ball either but Sewell needed a change. His plan worked.

Demaree slammed two hits and knocked in a run and Zarilla ripped a triple that knocked in two insurance runs in the twelveth inning of a 7-3 victory.

The following day St. Louis and Boston split their doubleheader. Muncrief pitched well for six innings in the opener but with his teammates' bats still silent he was forced to pitch too carefully and the Red Sox scored four in the seventh to take the game 5-1. In the nightcap, Jakucki didn't really have it but the Browns' bats woke up from a long sleep and pounded out a 12-8 triumph.

But just when it seemed the Browns might begin hitting, they were pounded 12-1 in the series finale. No one could blame the pitching staff for their surrendering twenty-five runs in the last three games. When a pitcher is forced to throw a shutout every game he's not going to be able to throw his game and sometimes loses total control of it. Sewell only hoped that the last three games would not be a sign of things to come.

The team was 16-12, half a game behind the front running Yankees and Senators, as they headed for Yankee Stadium. "The House That Ruth Built" was never a friendly place for the Browns to visit. Over the past decade they had lost 78 of 105 games played in New York.

Before departing on the railroad, Bill DeWitt informed rarely used outfielder Floyd Baker that he would be going to Toledo. This move, though inconspicuous at the time, was important in that it brought a key player to the Browns historic season. His name was Chet Laabs.

ONE CHAMPIONSHIP SEASON

Laabs would be available for night and weekend home games as well as night and weekend games in Cleveland, Chicago, and Detroit. He had been working in the Chrysler plant in Detroit but was given the okay to begin work in a plant in St. Louis which manufactured bombers. Because he had expected to be inducted into the army, he never reported to spring training. His spring training would have to take place during the course of the season.

Laabs began his major league career with the Detroit Tigers in 1937 when manager Mickey Cochrane brought him up to platoon with Jo Jo White in centerfield. He only hit .240 (six points less than White) but slugged eight home runs. His problem was that he was either hit or miss as he struckout 66 times in only 242 at bats. The following season his totals were almost the same before being traded to the Browns.

Laabs wasn't ecstatic about being traded to St. Louis but he was afforded an opportunity to play regularly. He hit .300 for the rest of 1939 before slumping to .271 in '40. His power totals increased to fifteen homers and twenty-three doubles in '41 before having his best season in '42. He finished with the fifth best slugging percentage in the league (.498), he was second to Ted Williams in home runs (27), and he knocked in 99 runs. He, like the whole Browns team, slumped in '43. Laabs struckout 105 times and knocked out only 17 home runs, but many more balls were falling short of the distant outfield fences because of a new baseball.

In 1943 baseball, because of a shortage of rubber, used a new substance called "balata." When home run production around the league had dropped seriously - there were only nine home runs in the American League after seventy-two games - the old baseballs were brought back into production.

As the '44 season got underway it looked like Laabs would be playing for the army instead of the Browns, but draft rulings delayed his induction and he was afforded another shot at playing.

It was only mid-May, but this series already was very significant. One team's domination could destroy the other's confidence if not for the rest of the season then enough to send them into a serious tailspin.

Going into the series the Browns found themselves shorthanded. McQuinn's sore left shoulder hurt enough for him to miss the first two games of the series and Kreevich was confined to the hotel room with a high fever.

Kreevich's illness allowed Zarilla another start in his place. He wasted no time in proving he belonged in the lineup by hitting a home run in the first inning to give the Browns a quick lead.

The lead was built to 3-0 in the second when Hayworth doubled in two runs but that didn't last as Potter ran into trouble in the bottom half of the second. After Snuffy Stirnweiss drove in the Yankees first run, Bud Metheny smoked a three-run homer and the Browns were suddenly behind 4-3. Potter got out of the inning without any further damage and settled down the rest of the way as St. Louis scored a run in the fourth on a passed ball, a run in the sixth on Byrnes' single, and what proved to be the winning run in the eighth, a home run by Christman.

The opening game victory seemed like a good step forward. The Browns regained first place by half a game and had their chance to show the Yankees that they were for real. Instead the Yankees showed the Browns just how good they were, even without their stars.

The next afternoon Kramer was beaten for the second time in a row when the Browns failed to hit for him. A St. Louis rally failed in the ninth and the Browns lost 3-2. Zar-

Jack Kramer is thrown out at the plate against the Yankees.
(The Bettman Archive)

illa was stranded at third in the ninth when Moore failed to get the key hit.

The Browns wound up their seventeen game road trip by getting swept on the Sunday doubleheader before a huge crowd of 59,161.

In the opener the Browns took a 3-2 lead in the top of the twelveth. Muncrief, 0-6 lifetime vs. the Yankees, was still on the mound as New York came to bat in the bottom half of the inning. With one out, Stirnweiss singled. He then stole second and went to third on a wild pitch. Metheny then fouled out to Mancuso behind the plate to put the Yankees on the brink.

Ed Levy then doubled down the rightfield line to tie the game. Nick Etten was intentionally walked but Don Savage followed with a dribbler to third. Christman raced in but had no play and suddenly the Yankees had the bases loaded. Sewell wasted no more time and brought Caster in from the bullpen.

Johnny Lindell stepped up to plate and decided to wait for his pitch. It never came as Caster walked him on five pitches. The Yankee Stadium crowd roared as the Browns slowly walked off the field. It was only May but there was a feeling for the Browns that things were beginning to slip away. St. Louis was never in the second game as the Yankees easily won 8-1 and increased their lead over the Browns to two and a half games. Only three games separated the Browns from last place, a position they were all too familiar with.

The team limped home losers of twelve of seventeen on the trip. The train ride back to Missouri was quiet. Sewell's men had two days off but the manager wanted them to re-port to Sportsman's Park the day before the beginning of a nineteen-game homestand to get plenty of batting practice.

While Sewell was trying to work with an injured force (Hayworth had a broken finger and Christman and Gut-teridge were suffering from bruised hands) he was relieved to find out that Kreevich, whose fever was diagnosed as influ-enza, and McQuinn, whose sore shoulder and back seemed to be on the mend, would be returning to the lineup.

While Kreevich was equally as important to the team as McQuinn, the loss of the St. Louis first baseman might have been severely damaging to the team's chances at their first pennant. McQuinn was the glue of the infield, one of the finest fielding first sackers to ever play the game.

McQuinn had spent seven years in the Yankees farm sys-tem while Lou Gehrig owned his position. Barnes and DeWitt had tried for years to acquire him but the Yankees

*George McQuinn is one of the most underrated fielding
first basemen of all time. (AP/Wide World Photo)*

used him as their insurance policy in case Gehrig went down.
While that may have been a good business decision, it was
damaging to McQuinn's psyche. Even after great seasons in
the minors he was never even invited to the Yankees spring
training camps. He eventually was sold to Cincinnati who
returned him to New York after he hit only .201 in 38
games.

When he was left available in the draft, the Browns grabbed him and in his first season with them (1938) he put together a 34-game hitting streak and finished the season with a .324 batting average. In his first four seasons with the Browns he averaged 16 homers, 85 runs batted in, and a .305 batting average. His totals slipped in '42 and '43 because of the worsening problem of his back. Still, he was a leader on the field and his leadership was needed.

The warm weather was upon St. Louis and it was hoped that there would be some thawing out of the bats. Of the 134 hits the team had gotten on the road trip, 103 were singles and that never did translate into run production.

A good crowd of 10,000 came out to Sportsman's Park to watch the return of their Browns. The team responded to the crowds enthusiasm by scoring three times in the first frame against the Red Sox. The key blow was a two run double by Christman.

The third baseman's bruised hand didn't stop him from hitting. His two-run double gave him ten runs batted in and a .281 batting average in his last seventeen games. Boston nicked Kramer for two runs before the Browns put the game away with a four-run fifth.

The following afternoon Muncrief had his first solid outing, holding on to win 3-2 and giving the Browns their first back-to-back wins since May 3rd and 4th against the Tigers.

Potter took the mound for the third game of the series. With the threat of rain in the air the crowd was a pretty good 7,000 plus. Dark clouds hovered around the park while the Browns scraped together two runs off Oscar Judd when Kreevich doubled home Gutteridge in the first and Gutteridge hit a sacrifice fly to score Demaree in the seventh.

Light raindrops splashed around the park as the Browns took the field in the eighth inning. Potter had been pitching

Nelson Potter (AP/Wide World Photo)

a great game and with the help of some great fielding behind him and a great mixing of his slider, screwball, and curve, he had set down the first twenty-one Red Sox to face him.

Slugger Bob Johnson and Bobby Doerr were retired easily to lead things off. Potter was now only four outs from a perfect game when Jim Tabor came to the plate. He had two strikes on him when he barely connected on the third pitch. The ball trickled under Potter's feet and towards the middle of the diamond. Gutteridge scrambled to get the ball and hurriedly threw the ball to first. Tabor beat the throw and the perfect game was lost. The next batter, Hal Wagner, walked, causing Mancuso to run out to the mound to settle down his pitcher. But on the first pitch to Skeeter Newsome, the shortstop lined a clean single to left breaking the shutout. Judd then struckout and Potter walked off the field with a 2-1 lead.

After rain halted play in the bottom of the eighth for twenty minutes, taking the steam out of a potential Browns rally, Potter surprisingly walked out to the mound. He had convinced Sewell that he was fine, but he quickly got into trouble.

After the first two batters singled, Joe Cronin hit a sacrifice fly to tie the game. Potter got out of the inning without further damage but pitched into the eleventh where he gave up two runs to lose the game. Only four outs from baseball immortality, he had to sit on his stool in front of his locker with sheer disappointment.

Behind Jakucki the Browns took the final game of the series thus winning three out of four. That was the kind of series they needed to prepare for the visit of the hated Yankees. The New Yorkers were not only hated by the other ballclubs but by the fans of the other ballclubs. Over 17,000 came to Sportsmans Park to watch the doubleheader which opened the series. Sewell threw Galehouse and Kramer at New York and watched as neither pitcher could contain the "starless" Yanks.

The aggravation of losing became quite evident when a case of "Yankee Favoritism" may have cost the team a possible victory in the opener. The Yankees had scored four runs in the top of the eleventh to take a 6-2 lead. The Browns in their half of the eleventh mounted a rally that brought home a run and left them with two men on base and two outs.

Kreevich then lined a shot into centerfield. The ball was hit so hard it began to sink sharply. Yankee centerfielder Johnny Lindell ran in and dove for the ball. The ball made its way into his mitt and he raised his gloved hand to indicate that he had caught it. Third base umpire Al Weafer signaled that Lindell made the catch but second base umpire Bill Grieve waved his hands saying the ball hit the ground first.

Gutteridge and West stood around the plate as they came around to score but they couldn't celebrate yet. The umpires decided to talk it over and when they ruled that the ball had been caught it brought about a round of boos from the fans and a vicious argument from Sewell and his men. Gutteridge had to be restrained by teammates as he went after Weafer. But as with all arguments the players never win and the Browns were forced to go back to the clubhouse and lick their "twin loss" wounds.

The team was now three and a half games behind the Yankees and in serious jeopardy of losing a grip on their season. The following day St. Louis showed the true spirit of a winner and trounced New York 11-3 with thirteen hits and home runs by McQuinn and Moore. There was no time to rest as the third place Senators came to town.

Washington, having been picked as one of the teams to contend with in the 1944 season, was having their problems getting untracked. They were only two games behind the second place Browns but they were already beginning the slide that would withdraw them from the pennant race.

Despite the slump they found themselves in, the Senators jumped out to a 3-0 lead by the fifth inning. Rain was beginning to fall heavily and the Browns were in jeopardy of losing a rain shortened game. In today's game the pitcher may take his time and hope the rain would come pouring down and suspend the game but in '44 players played with pride. If

George McQuinn is greeted by Vern Stephens (5) and Mike Kreevich (12) after slugging a home run. (The Bettman Archive)

a pitcher intentionally stalled, he'd be considered in the lowest of standards.

The Browns battled back to tie the game 3-3, and the rains fell almost as soon as the third out was made. After an hour delay Laabs hit his first home run of the season in the seventh to lead the Browns to a 6-4 win. In the nightcap, Shirley, who gave up seven walks, and Hollingsworth combined for a sloppy 4-2 win over a young Early Wynn.

The Browns ended the month of May with an exciting win that saw them tie the game with two runs in the ninth and win in the eleventh. The Senator killer was a former "Nat", Gene Moore. With the Browns down 3-2 with two out and Zarilla on third, Moore lined a shot into the left-centerfield gap for a triple tying the score. In the eleventh he hit a grounder between second and first which George Myatt dived for and stopped. But in his haste to make the throw, he threw the ball away and McQuinn scored the winning run. Combined with another Yankee loss at the hands of the Tigers, the Browns were now tied for first place.

In the final game of the series, Stan Spence went 6 for 6 as the Senators pounded Kramer and the Browns, 11-5. Sewell, with the knowledge that the Yankees had lost their fourth straight (opening the doors for the Browns to move into first place by percentage points), went through four pitchers - Kramer, West, Shirley, and Zoldak - in an effort to stay in the game.

The Browns got set to welcome the weak Athletics with the haunting remembrance of being swept by them at Shibe Park in early May. During a stretch that had seen the team go 12-16, the Browns not only found themselves not hitting but not pitching all that well either. The staff sported a 4.46 earned run average, a sharp contrast to the 2.73 earned run average they had in the team's first fifteen games.

Muncrief momentarily returned the Browns to pitching excellence with his fourth victory, a 3-0 shutout. All the runs he needed came in the second inning when Christman singled with the bases loaded to drive in two runs. Gutteridge followed with a run-scoring single.

Sewell and DeWitt's concern with the hitting grew with each low run-producing game. Both wondered when the Browns were going to unleash their offense. Then on the third day of June they slammed seventeen hits, including eight doubles and two home runs, against three pitchers in an 18-8 shellacking of Philadelphia. If there were a negative that day, it was Brownie pitching which surrendered seventeen hits.

Before having three days off, the Browns slammed twelve and then thirteen hits in their Sunday doubleheader split. Their bats now were alive as they amassed forty-six hits in the four game series which St. Louis took three games to one.

While the Browns relaxed before being visited by Cleveland, the Yankees were struggling and losing to the Red Sox. This created a two game lead that St. Louis hoped to increase while playing the seventh place Indians. But before the series began DeWitt was notified that his star relief pitcher, George Caster, had passed his military exam and would be called at some point by the Navy. Christman had also passed his exam; the Browns were left holding their breaths.

DeWitt spent a lot of time on the phone trying to work out a deal but the best he could do was sign Mike Chartak who left his Cleveland war plant job (a job he took when he didn't make the team in spring training).

The Browns lost the first three games of their series with Cleveland before Muncrief won his fourth in a row. Brownie bats went back to choking with men on base as the team scored only ten runs in the four game series. The most frustrating loss came on June 9th when the Browns got seventeen men to reach first (ten of whom made it to second) but scored only twice. The fact that they hit into only one doubleplay demonstrated their failure to hit in the clutch.

Players on the team were raising their averages, but without producing many runs. The Browns got the timely hit early in the year, but lost it during the recent road trip and homestand that followed.

Vern Stephens (5 HR, 30 RBI, .265 AVG) and George McQuinn (2 HR, 17 RBI, .276 AVG) continued to play solidly though they'd left their fair share of men on base. Milt

Byrnes (1 HR, 16 RBI, .275 AVG), Mike Kreevich (3 HR, 17 RBI, .264 AVG) and Gene Moore (3 HR, 26 RBI, .271 AVG) were giving St. Louis the best outfield in the league, offensively and defensively. Mark Christman (3 HR, 25 RBI, .283 AVG) was playing a fine third base and beginning to get a hot bat by hitting .371 in his last nine games. The same could be said of Don Gutteridge (0 HR, 11 RBI, .233 AVG). Frank Mancuso (1 HR, 9 RBI, .256 AVG) looked to be taking over the role behind the plate, especially after driving in six runs in the 18-8 beating of the Athletics, while Red Hayworth (0 HR, 6 RBI, .207 AVG) continued to struggle with his injured finger. The bench, which needs to be strong for a long season, was not supplying much as Harold Epps (.177), Al Zarilla (.143), and Toledo-bound Floyd Baker (.056) struggled with their few chances to play.

Despite the lack of offensive support, which altered the pitching game for most of the starting staff, the pitchers were doing well. Nelson Potter (5-4, 3.94 ERA)), Jack Kramer (7-5, 3.54 ERA), and Bob Muncrief (5-2, 3.00 ERA) were the anchors of the starting rotation. Various starts were given to Sig Jakucki (3-2, 4.75 ERA), Denny Galehouse (0-3, 4.85 ERA), Tex Shirley (2-3, 6.25 ERA), and the only lefthanded starter in Al Hollingsworth (2-2, 5.90 ERA). Each showed a flash of pitching brilliance but not enough consistency.

George Caster (2-2, 2.67 ERA, 3 Saves) continued to be the workhorse, coming out of the bullpen while lefties Lefty West (0-0, 6.43 ERA) and Sam Zoldak (0-0, 5.62 ERA) struggled in their minimal roles.

The time of the year when teams show if they are of championship caliber had arrived. There was still a lot of baseball left and all eight American League teams were still in the hunt.

June 12, 1944

	WON	LOST	GB
St. Louis Browns	28	23	—
Boston Red Sox	25	23	1½
Detroit Tigers	25	24	2
Chicago White Sox	22	22	2½
New York Yankees	22	22	2½
Cleveland Indians	24	26	3½
Philadelphia A's	22	24	3½
Washington Senators	22	26	4½

ONE CHAMPIONSHIP SEASON

CHAPTER 6

Winning In An Empty Park
(June 12 - July 9)

"The Browns pennant hopes will die late in July when the Missouri heat saps their pitching strength."

— Jimmy Dykes
(White Sox mgr.)

The Browns arrived in rainy Chicago early on the morning of June 12th. It was off to the hotel for a little rest before heading to Comiskey Park. Most were pleased to get the phone call that the game was cancelled but one player's message was not the same as the others. Frank Demaree's phone call came from DeWitt who informed the player that he was released. Demareee was hitting .255 but found himself odd man out in a crowded outfield.

With that unpleasant task done, DeWitt was notified by George Caster and Mark Christman that they had passed their military exam and expected to be called. Losing one or both of these men would have been a severe setback for the club but again "someone" was watching the St. Louis Browns and neither man was called.

Winners of four out of six against the White Sox, the Browns looked to get back on a winning track. But coming into the series the White Sox were hot, having won eight of nine. Their lone loss was a 1-0 shutout at the hands of Detroit. Their pitching staff had an earned run average of 1.89 during the run and the team was making a move.

Kramer looked to be on the verge of his fifth loss when with the help of some shoddy Chicago fielding, St. Louis rallied for three runs in the ninth inning and won 5-3. The victory was his eighth of the season but the first in two weeks.

Before a crowd of 24,893 on the next evening, the Browns continued their hitting when they racked two Chicago pitchers for sixteen hits in a 10-3 win. Zarilla banged out four hits and McQuinn slugged a homer in the barrage. The White Sox were beaten and never made noise again.

A day off for travel didn't cool the Browns' bats as they rose from eighth in the league to fifth in team batting when they battered the Tigers 14-1 and 5-0. The beneficiaries of the hitting were Muncrief (6-2) and Jakucki (4-2).

In the second game, Red Hayworth suffered another injury when he slid hard into third base in the ninth inning. Helped off the field with a twisted ankle, he relinquished the catching duties to Mancuso for the next two weeks.

With five consecutive victories and the rest of the league contenders struggling to play .500 ball, the Browns created a little distance from the rest of the pack. Still they had a Sunday doubleheader with Detroit before going back home. And pitching in the opening game was Hal Newhouser who always pitched well against the Browns when in Briggs Stadium.

Newhouser did not displease the 28,000 fans. He became the American League's first ten-game winner when he beat Kramer by a score of 7-3.

In the nightcap, St. Louis' Sunday pitcher Denny Galehouse again got hit hard and was out of the game by the fourth inning. He escaped his fourth consecutive loss when the Browns took a 5-3 lead but the bullpen failed Sewell's men.

Tex Shirley allowed the Tigers to tie the score in the fifth and then after three innings of one-hit relief, Nelson Potter succumbed to Detroit's bats when Rudy York slammed a game winning two-run homer. It was the fourth doubleheader that St. Louis had dropped.

The Browns took their one-game lead over the Red Sox home to host the third place White Sox. After a day of travel the Browns had to play their twelfth doubleheader in only two months of the season. A crowd of 11,877 flocked to the twilight doubleheader at Sportsman's Park to welcome their American League leaders home. They were treated to good baseball though their team only came away with a split.

Muncrief threw in the opener and pitched well enough to win but his own error cost him a victory. Leading 1-0 in the sixth he ran to cover first base on the back end of a doubleplay that was begun by McQuinn. St. Louis' fine first baseman was known as one of the best at fielding a grounder, throwing to second and getting back to first to receive a throw to complete a doubleplay. But as McQuinn raced back to first so did Muncrief. Both saw each other and stopped to allow the other to receive the ball. Stephens' throw whistled past both of them. Instead of an inning ending doubleplay, two runs crossed the plate.

The Browns did come back from the 3-1 deficit with solo runs in the eighth and ninth but with George Caster on the

Al Zarilla, George McQuinn, Vern Stephens & Mark Christman.
(The Bettman Archive)

mound in the tenth, Chicago's Ralph Hodgin lined a pitch off the screen in right field and Thurman Tucker came around from first to score what proved to be the winning run.

Hollingsworth sent the crowd home happy when he won his third consecutive game in the nightcap, tossing a five-hit shutout, 5-0. For only the fourth time in the past three weeks Mark Christman was held without knocking in a run. Since May 27th he had hit in 22 of 24 games with three home runs and twenty-two runs batted in. His run production thus far in the season had been a pleasant surprise for Sewell.

After DeWitt acquired him in the "big trade" with Detroit back in 1939 he hit only .216 for the Browns. He was sent to Toledo to work on pulling the ball and after improving with each passing year he finally stuck with the big club in '43. Sewell liked his aggressive style of play while he backed up starting third baseman Harlond Clift. At this point in the '44 season Christman had already equaled his run production of the year before and had become one of the better third basemen in the league. In '43 he handled 454 chances and bobbled only three of them.

The following afternoon the Browns won 11-2, marking the third time in a week they had scored ten or more runs. Moore's fourth and Stephens' seventh home runs of the season aided Potter's seventh victory.

Kramer was pitching fine until the eighth inning of the series finale when he was tagged for seven runs in a 10-3 loss. It was his seventh loss in his last ten decisions.

Despite splitting the four-game series, St. Louis had widened their lead to two games over Boston, three games over Chicago, and three-and-a-half games over their next visitors, Detroit.

Jakucki pitched like a man with somewhere to go as he disposed of Detroit in an hour and a half, posting his fifth win and second consecutive shutout. The Browns scored all five of their runs in the first two innings as they continued their dominance of Detroit.

The emergence of Sig Jakucki as a valuable pitcher was a surprise to almost everyone on the club. He was considered a long shot when a scout for St. Louis rediscovered him pitching against an Army team in '43. The hard-living pitcher had first pitched for the Browns in 1936 and was sent to the minors for the next two seasons. Unhappy with his situation and feeling the need to spread his wings, Jakucki joined a team that would travel the world and play teams from different countries. This led to starting assignments in China, the

Sig Jakucki (National Baseball Library
& Archive, Cooperstown, N.Y.)

Phillipines, Honolulu and finally in a shipyard in Galveston, Texas where he was spotted pitching against the Army.

Jakucki had a great sinking fastball that today would probably be called a split-finger fastball. He was a big man (6'3", 200 pounds) but he was a fine fielder, strengthening the Browns already well-balanced infield.

The following day Vern Stephens and Milt Byrnes helped the Browns bolster their lead over the Red Sox to three and a half games as they slapped seven hits between them. Muncrief earned his seventh victory, his sixth in a row.

Twelve thousand came to the park on Sunday to watch the Browns' hitters face two of the game's best pitchers in Detroit's Dizzy Trout and Hal Newhouser. Sewell elected to go with Potter and Hollingsworth instead of the usual weekend appearance by Galehouse. Galehouse had yet to win a game and only one of his six appearances was considered a good outing. Sewell wanted to use him in relief but he never got into either game.

Looking more and more like a team of desiny, the Browns won the opener when Byrne—in his second consecutive three hit game—doubled in the winning run in the tenth. The Browns had tied the game in the ninth on a two-run homer by McQuinn.

Newhouser never had a chance against St. Louis in the nightcap as they scored three times in the first and went on to win 52, enjoying their eleventh win in fourteen meetings against the Tigers. The sweep of Detroit opened a four game lead on the second place White Sox.

The Browns were certainly looking like a team destined to win the pennant, but their fans had a hard time realizing it. Through the first thirty-five home games, the Browns had attracted only 145,000 fans. By contrast, the last place Athletics had attracted 320,000 fans in the same time span. Some said that the gasoline restrictions hurt fans who had to drive a long way to the park. Others blamed the concessions (20¢ beer, 15¢ hot dogs, and 10¢ scorecards). Barnes openly questioned fan loyalty but left town with the team before hearing the displeasure St. Louis fans took to his statement.

The twenty-one hour train ride to New York was a pleasant one for the team as they took their recent success to

ONE CHAMPIONSHIP SEASON

Yankee Stadium to begin a twenty-game road trip. Sewell was in good spirits and was confident the team would not repeat the 5-12 east coast jaunt of earlier in the season. On the train with the team was Chet Laabs who had quit his war-plant job the day before to become a full member of the team.

Sewell was looking to have more power in the lineup. Laabs was finding it difficult to get into a groove when splitting his time between his job and baseball. His stats (1 HR, 3 RBI, .111 AVG.) attested to that. Leaving the war plant job did leave him open to the draft - he had already passed his physical - but with the prospects of the team getting to the World Series he was willing to take that chance.

The Yankees had never been kind to the Browns. Since 1922 the Browns had lost to the Yankees 326 times while winning only 155. The Browns had tied the season series with the Yankees only four times and lost 21 games out of 22 in 1927. Their only win came on the last day of that season.

The Yankees were expecting Hollingsworth or Kramer to go against them in the opener but Sewell selected seven game winner Bob Muncrief to take the mound. Muncrief had become the most consistent pitcher on the staff over the last four weeks, having won six in a row while compiling an awesome earned run average of 1.63 in eight appearances.

The streak of Muncrief's didn't impress the Yankees and they showed it by trouncing him 7-2. He was gone by the fourth inning and the Browns were unable to mount any threats against Atley Donald.

The game the following afternoon was a tough one to lose. Jakucki, who had thrown two consecutive shutouts, had another one going until the ninth inning. Unfortunately, the Browns had not scored either so Jakucki had no room for error.

With two out and a runner on second Sewell had the idea of walking Nick Etten so that weak-hitting Rollie Hemsley would be forced to bat. Hemsley drilled a pitch beyond the reach of Milt Byrnes in centerfield for a long single and a New York 1-0 victory.

Hollingsworth was determined to prevent a sweep and he pitched a great game. The Yankees could not get anything going as they hit into five doubleplays. In the middle of each of each those doubleplays was second baseman Don Gutteridge who set a then record for American League second sackers. Hollingsworth's seven-hit shutout combined with Stephens' first inning blast (extending his hitting streak to sixteen games during which he batted .463) guided St. Louis to a 3-0 victory. It was Hollingsworth's fourth victory of June against no defeats but it would be his last of the season.

The Browns marched into Fenway Park for their biggest series of the season. The Red Sox were only two and a half games behind and they were almost unbeatable at home, having won seventeen of nineteen home games.

The Browns took the opener 9-1, giving Potter his eighth win, but the Sox took the doubleheader the following day. The Browns lost their second 1-0 game in less than a week before blowing a two run lead in the nightcap.

Tex Shirley was pitching a three hitter and had a 3-1 lead going into the bottom of the ninth. With one out he surrendered a long double to Bob Johnson and Bobby Doerr came to the plate. Sewell wasted no time in getting a fresh arm in there as he called on Bob Muncrief. Muncrief had only pitched four innings in the past week.

Muncrief got Doerr to ground out. Up came Lou Finney, batting for the first time in the major leagues in two years. He had replaced Joe Cronin who had gotten himself thrown out of the game an inning earlier.

*George McQuinn is tagged out at the plate by
Boston's Joe Wood after a wild pitch. Bob
Muncrief looks on. (Missouri Historical Society)*

Finney managed to get enough of the ball to pop it just
inside the leftfield line out of Byrnes' reach. One run scored
and Finney reached second. Hal Wagner followed with a single to right and the game was tied and going into extra innings.

Muncrief allowed a leadoff double in the eleventh and
after getting the next batter out elected to walk Doerr. This
set up the chance for an inning ending doubleplay with Finney again stepping to the plate. He grounded hard to Gutteridge at second but the ball rolled right through his legs
into rightfield and the winning run came around to score.

The Browns had lost four of six, and the Red Sox were
now only a game and a half back. The skeptics were waiting

for St. Louis to fold but the Browns were on to Philadelphia, hopeful to raise their level of play.

An Independence Day doubleheader attracted 23,858 patriotic fans as the teams split the twinbill. The Athletics were in the basement but only eight games out, so no one on that team felt they were merely playing out the season. Jakucki threw his third shutout in four starts to start things off. He had given up only one run in his last thirty-seven innings, a phenomenal run. Christman led the attack with his fifth home run of the season.

Former Brownie Bobo Newsom on the mound for Philadelphia in the opener was frustrated that his team was not scoring any runs for him. To make matters worse, Sewell was on the coaching lines at third heckling the pitcher. Newsom turned and fired the ball in the manager's direction. Though the ball didn't come close to hitting Sewell, the heckling subsided.

In the nightcap, Hollingsworth was rattled for five runs in four innings of an 8-3 loss.

The final two games of the series were well played. The Athletics had come back to tie the Browns 2-2 when St. Louis pulled it out in the ninth. Pitcher George Caster singled in two runs to land himself a victory and in the final game Bob Muncrief threw a four-hit shutout after retiring the first fourteen batters in the game. It was his eighth win in twelve decisions.

The Browns left for Washington still leading the Red Sox by two and a half games. The Yankees were still close at three and a half while the Senators were fourth, five games out.

Before beginning the first game of the series the Senators and Browns and a host of others enjoyed the festivities of a war relief contest. The game netted a little more than

$17,000 for war relief organizations. Players, umpires, and sportswriters paid their own way into the stadium. The fans were treated to the antics of baseball clown, Nick Altrock, greats like Walter Johnson, Muddy Ruel, and a member of the Senators 1933 championship team, Luke Sewell. Members of the Browns and Senators competed in races with the winners receiving $50 war bonds. It was the last time these two teams did anything friendly together. By the heat of the summer they would be at each other's throats, literally.

The Browns had lost two of three in their last visit to Griffith Stadium so it was with a little extra incentive that they attack the Senators. Unfortunately Kramer had nothing on his pitches and was done in easily, 7-0. The loss dropped his record to 8-9.

Sewell worried about his star pitcher. He had lost his last outing 1-0 but in the five games surrounding that outing he had lost four of five decisions with a 6.46 earned run average. But the All-Star break was almost upon them and Kramer would be able to get a week's rest before the Browns were to embark on the most important part of the season.

Jakucki (6-3) took the mound the following evening. He was on a streak that had seen him allow only one run in his last thirtyeight innings of work. The lone run surrendered came in a 1-0 loss.

There would be no shutout on this day as Washington pushed across three runs in the first two innings. It was a sloppily played game - four errors for Washington and three for St. Louis - but the Browns took advantage of the ones afforded them and came away with a 5-4 win. Centerfielder Milt Byrnes, moving over from his usual spot in leftfield to give Kreevich a rest, led the attack with a triple and two singles while Laabs had three hits.

Jack Kramer (National Baseball Library
& Archive, Cooperstown, N.Y.)

The Sunday doubleheader was split when Tex Shirley tossed a shutout in the opener, 10-0, allowing Washington only two singles before knuckleballer Dutch Leonard dazzled St. Louis 4-0.

The Browns had reached the half way point in the season, two and a half games up on the Red Sox and three and a half games up on the Yankees. While the team headed for Toledo to play an exhibition game before getting a couple of days off, George McQuinn (5 HR, 31 RBI, .265), major league runs batted in leader Vern Stephens (9 HR, 54 RBI, .302), and Bob Muncrief (8-4, 2.92) headed for Pittsburgh to represent the Browns in the All-Star Game.

Like every All-Star game, some deserving player is over-looked. Mark Christman (5 HR, 44 RBI, .301) was such a player but Cleveland's Ken Keltner (.260) was given the nod at third.

The Browns had won twelve of their last twenty and seemed to be clicking. The infield was on top of their game defensively and each man filling in in the oufield was doing his job admirably.

Don Gutteridge (0 HR, 16 RBI, .231) was letting his hustle speak for himself while Mike Kreevich (4 HR, 25 RBI, .296), Gene Moore (4 HR, 40 RBI, .253), and Milt Byrnes (2 HR, 29 RBI, .277) continued their steady play in the outfield.

Outfielders Al Zarilla (1 HR, 10 RBI, .211), Chet Laabs (1 HR, 4 RBI, .207), and Mike Chartak (1 for 12) would figure prominently later in the season while they slowly got themselves in shape for their assault on American League pitching.

If anything was still bothering the St. Louis front office it was the catching. Red Hayworth (0 HR, 12 RBI, .235) and Frank Mancuso (1 HR, 17 RBI, .217) were playing their best through injuries. Mancuso's back was restricting his ability to catch pop ups, and Hayworth was getting banged around so much (finger, ankle, back) that he looked like a wounded war hero. It didn't help Barnes to know that former Brownie catchers Rick Ferrell and Frankie Hayes were members of the All-Star team.

The one constant on the team was the pitching. While Muncrief's pitching got him a ticket to the All-Star Game, the pitching of Sig Jakucki (7-3, 2.53), Nelson Potter (8-5, 3.20), Jack Kramer (8-9, 3.99) and George Caster (3-3, 3.44, 4 SV) was nothing short of superb. Al Hollingsworth (5-4, 3.77) who at one point looked like a valuable man in the starting rotation, damaged his status by losing his last two. Denny Galehouse (0-3, 4.09) still needed to pitch himself into shape while seldom used Sam Zoldak (5.50) and Lefty West (7.26) would not figure much for the rest of the season.

The dog days of summer were officially upon the players. The hot Missouri heat would do its best to wilt the strenght of its hometown players but Sewell was a master of playing them when they were hot and resting them when they were not.

ONE CHAMPIONSHIP SEASON

July 10, 1944

	WON	LOST	GB
St. Louis Browns	45	34	—
Boston Red Sox	42	36	2½
New York Yankees	39	35	3½
Washington Senators	38	39	6
Chicago White Sox	34	37	7
Cleveland Indians	37	41	7½
Detroit Tigers	36	42	8½
Philadelphia A's	35	42	9

CHAPTER 7

Pulling Ahead
(July 13 - August 12)

"Let's not forget, the last fifty games are certain to be the hardest."

- Wray's Column,
St. Louis Post Dispatch

Not only did the Browns have to work during part of their break, losing to Toledo in major league baseball's continued good will effort to bring major leagues to minor league cities, but Sportsman's Park didn't get a breather either. Both the Browns and Sportsman's Park continued doing their part to unite Americans and promote harmony. Ten thousand spectators crammed the field to watch actor Don Ameche and the great American poet Langston Hughes partake in a music festival to promote interracial good will.

Only the year before there had been race riots in Detroit, Los Angeles, and in Beaumont, Texas. Instead of the horrible presence of the National Guard, which Briggs Stadium hired to keep the peace, Sportsman's Park held a festival occasion that had everyone smiling upon leaving.

This festival was not the first bringing together of both races in Sportsman's Park. When the season began the practice of seating African-Americans in the rightfield pavilion seats, behind a giant screen, was abolished. They were now able to purchase any ticket in the park. America was slowly beginning to change and so was baseball.

The Detroit Tigers momentum also changed. Returning from the Naval Air Corps was Dick Wakefield, who as a rookie in 1943 had led the league in doubles (38), hits (200), and batting average (.316). Chuck Hostetler, a fine backup, had not been able to replace Wakefield's bat.

McQuinn, Muncrief, and Stephens met the rest of the team in Cleveland where they were to begin the second half of the season with a six-game series. The Brownie all-stars all appeared in the "mid-summer classic" with McQuinn and Stephens both getting singles while Muncrief pitched a scoreless inning and a third. Despite the positive stats the National League won 7-1.

The Indians hardly played like a team in sixth place as they took three of four from the Browns. They rattled Jakucki in the opener, won a squeaker in fourteen innings, and crushed Hollingsworth 13-2.

Dropping three of the first four was only one worry for Sewell. The fourteen-inning loss was the result of a throwing error by Stephens. After the game the shortstop sat by his locker rubbing his elbow. The elbow had bothered him for some time but he failed to let anyone know about it until the pain was excrutiating. Bob Bauman worked feverishly on Stephens but Sewell decided to play it safe and bench him for a while. Losing Stephens for a long period of time would certainly do damage to the Browns' pennant hopes. It would be a week before he would start another game.

While the Browns were losing three of four, the Yankees were beating the Red Sox two of three and moving into second place, one game and a half out. The Yankees were also blessed with the good news that shortstop Frank Crosetti was rejoining the team. This had Yankee beat writers penciling in New Yorkers for a comeback. Cleveland writers were already labeling St. Louis, "the sliding Browns."

The largest crowd of the season (32,553) at Municipal Stadium watched the Sunday doubleheader, the final games of the series. The Browns had now been the visitors at the largest attendance getters in New York, Washington, Boston, and now Cleveland. It pleased Donald Barnes to see there was interest in his team outside of St. Louis. But again the question was raised as to why the Browns did not attract but a couple of thousand to their home games. This was a point of discussion with many of the Browns' players who were drawing large crowds on the road.

The opening game of the doubleheader looked dim as the Browns blew a 7-4 lead when the Indians scored two in the eighth and one in the ninth. The strong pitching of the first half of the season disappeared. Tex Shirley, Lefty West, and George Caster walked fifteen men and surrendered ten hits. McQuinn's game-winning single in the twelfth momentarily erased the poorness of the outing.

Jack Kramer threw in the nightcap and he pitched excellent ball for twelve innings, winning when Milt Brynes hit a sacrifice fly to score Gutteridge.

The Browns finished the long road trip by splitting the twenty games and still held a two-game lead over the Yankees as they headed home to host their closest competitors.

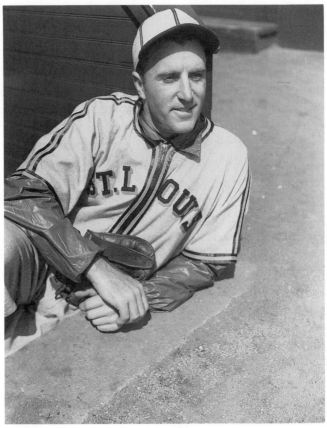

*Denny Galehouse left his war plant job when he saw the
Browns had a shot at the pennant. (The Bettman Archive)*

The pitching staff had not been impressive during the
Cleveland series (with the exception of Muncrief and Kramer) and the Browns needed a couple of healthy arms in the
rotation to help the tiring ones along. Barnes was unable to
make any kind of trade but he did convince Denny Galehouse to take a leave of absense from his war plant job in
Akron, Ohio. With steady work he was destined to improve
on his 0-3 record.

The players' and ownership voicing of displeasure about attendance was loud enough for the St. Louis fans to respond. Then again it didn't hurt that it was the Yankees in town. For once Barnes' hopes were realized as over 60,000 fans came out for the four game series. Almost 20,000 showed up for the opener to witness Muncrief toss an 8-0 shutout for his ninth win. Home runs by Laabs, Byrnes, and Moore, which all cleared the rightfield pavilion, accounted for seven of the runs.

The following evening Jakucki sought to avenge the 1-0 loss he took at the hands of the Yankees at the end of June. But the big man was still being troubled by a strained muscle in his back and for the second consecutive start he was rattled and lost 6-5. This one hurt a little more because he had been spotted a 5-2 lead when he surrendered a three-run homer to hard-hitting Johnny Lindell in the sixth inning.

The biggest game of the series occurred on the twentieth of July and not even the Browns' victory overshadowed what happened in that game.

Potter took the mound for game three against twelve-game winner Hank Borowy on a surprisingly cool dry night. There was no score after three and a half innings when the trouble started.

As the Yankees took the field Sewell walked out of the dugout towards home plate umpire Cal Hubbard and suggested that he inform Borowy to stop moistening his fingers. Sewell didn't like the look of a couple of pitches and felt a spitball was being used.

Borowy didn't seem bothered by the request but when Hubbard walked back to the plate, Yankees third base coach Art Fletcher, yelling from the dugout, wanted to know what the problem was. Hubbard made a detour and walked to the mouth of the Yankees dugout. He explained the complaint made by Sewell but whereas Borowy wasn't affected by the request, Fletcher and McCarthy were. They thought Potter was the one throwing a spitter.

The inning was resumed and Hubbard made his way to the mound at the same time as Potter. Hubbard told Potter to stop blowing in his clenched fist and Potter, though surprised by the request, agreed. The problem was that this action was just a reflex for Potter. He always had a habit of blowing in his fist before picking up the resin bag so that he could get a good grip on the ball. His reflex got the best of him as he went to his mouth before throwing the first pitch of the evening.

Hubbard yanked off his mask and walked to the mound. Sewell raced out to intercept him and got into a mild arguement with the umpire. Potter was annoyed with the situation and then sealed his fate when play was set to resume. He looked in for the sign and then exaggeratedly licked his fingers. Hubbard threw his right arm in the air and Potter was ejected. Sewell again raced for the mound and argued long and loud enough to be ejected as well.

The 13,000 usually subdued midwesterners got loud and angry at their best pitcher's ejection and soon the outfield was filled with soda bottles.

Potter took his case to the league president and the commissioner, contending that he was not and had no intention of throwing a spitball. Going to his mouth was just an old habit of his. His plea fell on deaf ears and American League President Will Harridge suspended him for ten days.

Potter's case was almost thrown out before it could be listened to because at various times during the season other managers (Lou Boudreau, Joe Cronin, and Connie Mack) had openly complained that they suspected the pitcher of throwing the illegal pitch. Since Potter had pitched under

Mack for the Athletics from 1938-41 as well as Cronin for the Red Sox in '41, the inside scoop was that the pitcher was caught by his mentors.

Potter was scheduled to return on August first but the Browns had trouble locating him. He had gone back home and enjoyed the relaxation so much that he forgot his due date. He showed up almost a week late. By season's end it was obvious that this suspension and/or his lateness cost him a twenty win season.

The Browns blew the game open in the seventh and went home with a 7-3 win, including Galehouse's first win of the season, but the aggravation that another call had gone the way of the Yankees knawed at each and every Brown.

The following day Hollingsworth was hit hard as the Yankees took the game 8-2, allowing them to leave town with a split of the series. The poor outing by the lefthander (in his last four games he netted an 11.25 earned run average) banished him to the bullpen. Everyone in the Browns front office knew his arm was a ticking time bomb. He had been classified as 4-F by the military because they found bone chips in his elbow, to go along with his bad ankles. The fact that he threw two shutouts during the season (one against Chicago and the other against the Yankees) showed the courage and competitiveness of the lefthander. But his injury would reduce his pitching to just sixteen innings the rest of the season.

The Missouri heat and humidity were climbing as the Red Sox came to town. Blocks of ice with fans blowing behind them were set up on each side of both dugouts to cool off the players. Plenty of water was available to keep the pitchers from dehydrating. It wasn't much relief as Kramer and Muncrief, Sewell's two hottest pitchers, were blown out of the first two games (8-4 and 12-1, resepectively) marking only the third time that season the Browns had lost three in a row.

Sewell didn't like what he saw. Since the all-star break the Browns had lost seven of twelve. The pitchers were being batted around (5.66 earned run average in that span) and the hitting, which had heated up before the break, was cold again. He spoke about how he was going to be platooning more during the summer months to keep everyone from getting stiff on the bench. He was going to go with the hot hand or bat and sit the cool players for a while.

The first such move was the benching of Chet Laabs who was in the midst of an 0 for 15 slump. The struggling outfielder took his .204 batting average to the bench in favor of Al Zarilla who had gone three weeks without a start. He was hitting no better than Laabs but Sewell liked what he saw during batting practice.

Zarilla aided Jakucki and Galehouse in their victories over the Red Sox in the final two games of the series and almost singlehandedly eliminated Philadelphia and Washington from the pennant race as he hit three home runs, knocked in fifteen runs, and batted over .500. He had six multi-hit games including four games where he had three hits in each. But a sign that Zarilla, Sewell, and the rest of the Browns were a team of destiny came during a game against the Athletics.

With the Browns taking a 6-5 lead into the seventh, Zarilla stepped to the plate against Don Black with a man on. First base umpire Bill McGowan yelled time while Moore was tying his shoe laces. But Black and Zarilla never heard him. Zarilla lined the pitch to rightfield where outfielder Bobby Estalella caught the ball. As the Athletics started running in, McGowan was still waving his arms. There was a short argument from the Athletics but Zarilla returned to the batters box. The first pitch by Black was slammed over the

*During an 11-game hitting streak, Al Zarilla had seven
multi-hit games. (The Bettman Archive)*

rightfield pavilion and the Browns were up 8-5 instead of
clinging to a one-run lead going into the eighth.

The Browns took three of four from the Athletics but
still couldn't distance themselves from Boston or New York.
It wasn't until the Senators came to town for four games
while the Yankees faced the hot Tigers and the Red Sox
faced the troublesome Indians that the Browns created a little more than breathing room.

The opening game of the series with Washington almost
started on a tragic note. The first game was rained out but a
rough wind storm preceded the rain.

Mark Christman and Vern Stephens had stepped from
the dugout to have a catch when a gust of wind ripped a
heavy piece of timber from the grandstand roof. Neither

player saw it hurtling through the air and it crashed at Christman's feet. It understandably shook up the third baseman, and both men retired to the clubhouse.

An injury to Christman would have been devastating to the team. Sewell was worried about his substitute infielders who were for the most part unrested. Only Ellis Clary and Floyd Baker were able to replace any of the four, and both were very weak at the plate.

Before shopping for an extra infielder, Barnes purchased a new catcher, Tom Turner, from the White Sox. Turner was hitting .230 for Chicago when Barnes acquired him, but he was healthy. Red Hayworth and Frank Mancuso were hurting badly and both were in need of some rest. Hayworth was hitting only .161 in July while Mancuso was hitting .176 during the same stretch. Joe Schultz who was down on the farm in Toledo had suffered an injury and was unavailable for call-up.

The Senators had lost seven straight and thirteen of seventeen since the All-Star break. They had played themselves right out of the pennant race but they were not going to bow easily to the Browns. The two teams did not get along and it would be more of a pleasure to the Senators to beat the Browns than it would to beat the Yankees.

Muncrief pitched a great game in the opener but so did Washington's Mickey Haefner as both matched zeros for nine innings. Washington scored one run in the tenth and looked to break their losing streak.

After Zarilla and Christman led off with outs, Mancuso kept things alive with a single to left. Tom Hafey was sent in to pinch hit for Muncrief and walked.

Sewell wanted some speed on the base paths so he sent Shirley in to run for Hafey. Gutteridge came to bat and with two strikes slammed a pitch into the farthest part of right-centerfield. Mancuso came in to score easily and Shirley made it to the plate without a throw as the Browns won, 2-1. Denny Galehouse won his third in a row in a 7-3 contest in the nightcap.

St. Louis extended Washington's losing streak to eleven with two more wins in the next two days. During the series Don Gutteridge's bat came alive (.474) as he extended his hitting streak to fourteen games. The acquisition of Gutteridge by Sewell and DeWitt was another in the line of "genius" moves the two made. The scrappy second baseman began his career with the Cardinals but threatened to quit baseball when the National League team sent him to the minors after using him mainly as a pinch hitter during the 1940 season. He was a third baseman for the Cardinals and his position was given to Stu Martin when the team brought up prospect Joe Orengo. Gutteridge was sent to Sacramento of the Pacific Coast League where, despite putting up fantastic numbers (he hit .309, with 31 doubles, 13 triples, 46 stolen bases and 113 runs scored in 171 games), he threatened to retire from baseball if he wasn't brought up. The Browns scouts took notice of his PCL stats and acquired him on a "look-see" basis. After watching Gutteridge play third base, Sewell remarked how lousy he was at the position. The Browns' manager tried the youngster at second, making it home for the rest of his career.

The Browns now had a five and a half game lead on Boston, six and a half on New York, and seven and a half on Cleveland. St. Louis fans took notice of the Browns as over 30,000 turned out for the four-game series with the last place Senators. While that still wasn't good it was an improvement.

After concluding their homestand with a three-game sweep of the third place Indians (before an average of 16,000 fans), the Browns were not only getting local support but national attention. The team was pulling away from the pack, and east coast writers were worried.

On the train ride from St. Louis to New York the Browns caught drift of an article by John Drebinger of the *New York Times* who wrote that "baseball is rushing towards a World Series no one wants to see." He went on to criticize St. Louis fans for not turning out to see the Browns. What he failed to research was that over 100,000 men were serving in the military in an area that did not have the population of Manhattan, much less the New York metropolitan area. Of course the rest of the article went on to boast about the Yankees attendance. Brownie players brushed it off. No one had believed in them all season long so it didn't matter to them if baseball fans' minds changed or not.

They arrived in Yankee Stadium to begin their final extended road trip (twenty-two games) with an eight-game winning streak, a six and a half game lead on second place, and possession of first place for a team record seventy consecutive days.

Thinking they had escaped the August humidity in Missouri, the Browns found themselves in an even muggier New York City. The hitters were looking tired in the opener as Hank Borowy had them down 2-1 going into the top of the eighth inning.

With one out and runners on first and third, Mike Kreevich ripped a shot into rightfield. Playing shallow, Yankees rightfielder Bud Metheny ran back as fast as he could before finally leaping as high as he could, catching and robbing Kreevich of a three run homer. Tex Shirley tagged up to tie the game but Metheny drew wild applause as he temporarily saved the game.

But in the ninth Zarilla tagged one deep. So deep that Metheny didn't bother to move and the Browns took the

Al Zarilla's fifth home run helped defeat the Yankees 3-2.
(AP/Wide World Photo)

opener 3-2 as Jakucki, sent to the bullpen to work on his pitching, saved his second consecutive game.

The Browns broke their own season record when they made it ten in a row the following day as Galehouse won his fifth in a row, a 3-0 shutout. Despite the win another injury was sustained by the catching corp. Tom Turner, who was getting some playing time and benefitting from it (six hits in ten at bats), injured on a foul tip. The injury worsened the problem, at the Browns weakest position. Turner would bat only seventeen more times the rest of the season.

Sewell decided to go with Jakucki for the third game of the series because the righthander had looked good in his two relief appearances and had only pitched in four innings in the past ten days. But he didn't get past the fifth inning as the Yankees defeated the Browns to end their ten-game winning streak.

The Browns bid adieu to New York City with an 8-3 victory behind Kramer's twelveth win and McQuinn's two homers, his eighth and ninth of the season.

Players were looking sluggish at the plate so Sewell gave everyone resting time, even if it meant starting someone and yanking him after five innings.

The infield, however, seemed fresh as Stephens (11 HR, 73 RBI, .295), Christman (5 HR, 59 RBI, .288), and Gutteridge (0 HR, 23 RBI, .254) were still playing superb baseball. Gutteridge was hitting .316 during the past month and a half, adding to his aggressive play on the field. McQuinn's bat (9 HR, 55 RBI, .262) was slipping a little with each passing month but his fielding wasn't.

In the outfield, Sewell was working his magic. Kreevich (4 HR, 36 RBI, .299) remained the constant out there while Byrnes (3 HR, 35 RBI, .297), Moore (5 HR, 49 RBI, .238) and Laabs (2 HR, 11 RBI, .207) were platooned around Al Zarilla's (5 HR, 30 RBI, .285) hot bat. Zarilla's production was impressive considering he had only 172 at bats.

The Browns thought they had solved their catching problem but recently acquired Tom Turner (6 for 10) went down with an injury when he took a foul on his thumb. Hayworth (1 HR, 16 RBI, .226) and Mancuso (1 HR, 23 RBI, .210) were going to have to pick things up.

Potter (10-5, 3.00), Kramer (12-10, 2.69), Muncrief (12-6, 2.58), and Jakucki (9-7, 3.91) were pitching well. Caster (5-3, 2.18, 7 saves) was taking care of the bullpen with help from Shirley (4-3, 4.10). Hollingsworth (5-6, 4.38) was questionable for the rest of the season and Galehouse (5-3, 2.55) was pitching the kind of ball that Sewell knew he could.

Having built a big lead, the players started openly talking about what they were going to do with their World Series share. Their play became too relaxed, and they began playing less than .500 baseball. All the while, no one was paying attention to the hot Detroit Tigers.

ONE CHAMPIONSHIP SEASON

August 13, 1944

	WON	LOST	GB
St. Louis Browns	65	43	—
Boston Red Sox	58	49	6½
Detroit Tigers	56	50	8
New York Yankees	54	51	9½
Cleveland Indians	53	57	13
Chicago White Sox	51	56	13½
Philadelphia A's	49	61	17
Washington Senators	44	63	20½

CHAPTER 8

Losing Grip
August 13 - September 10

"There isn't any pressure on us. It's all on the other clubs. We can lose a couple of games here and there and still be all right."

— Luke Sewell

From the first day in spring training till the final day of the season, Sewell continually talked pennant to the Browns. But knowing that the dog days of August bred disinterest in players - especially Browns players who didn't know what it was like to be in a pennant race this late in the season - the talk took a back seat to his ability to get everyone in the lineup.

Sewell did an excellent job by constantly changing the lineup and platooning players so that everyone felt a part of the team. His moves were working but for the next four weeks exhaustion was weakening the Browns.

Boston was closest to catching the Browns but though they split the four game series and remained six and a half games back, they were dealt a blow that knocked them out of the race.

The draft board ordered pitcher Tex Hughson (18 wins), catcher Hal Wagner (.330), and second baseman Bobby Doerr (.325) (number one and two in the American League batting race, respectively) to report for military duty effective in a few weeks. They kept Boston in the picture until departing.

But Al Zarilla also received a telegram from the Army. He was given notice that he had to report for duty three weeks before the season would end. Alarmed, DeWitt raced to the induction center to speak with the board. Zarilla had been the team's best hitter for the past month, batting an even .500 with four home runs and nineteen runs batted in. His loss in the lineup could have been devastating. Luckily DeWitt was able to postpone the induction until mid-October.

Thirteen-game winner Bob Muncrief, who was 4-0 with a 2.38 earned run average in his last five appearances, was chosen to pitch the opener. After Muncrief was staked to a 5-1 lead by the fourth inning the Red Sox' bats came alive. The Brownie pitcher was knocked out when the Sox tied the game. Caster came on in relief and, despite a 6-5 lead in the ninth, failed to hold Boston down. Boston finally won in the thirteenth.

St. Louis won the second game, courtesy of a rain shortened game, but lost 5-1 the following day when Galehouse lost his first game in two months. Making the series a little brighter was Vern Stephens who hit a grand slam in the series finale to put the Browns on the winning side.

For the past month the Browns had gained on every team but one. The Detroit Tigers played the same ball the Browns were playing in the same time span. Hal Newhouser and Dizzy Trout were working at a pace that made everyone think the Detroit pitching staff consisted of only the two men. They already had nineteen wins apiece at this point in the season. The addition of Dick Wakefield (5 HR, 20 RBI, .295 AVG. in a little more than a month) fueled Detroit's already lethal offense. Winners of twenty of twenty-eight, the Tigers would show absolutely no sign of slowing up. Their head to head play with St. Louis was still two weeks away.

Still holding a six and a half game lead on their closest rivals, the Browns headed for Philadelphia to play the 51-63 Athletics. After bowing to Philadelphia in their first three meetings of the season, St. Louis had beat them in nine of their last twelve. The Athletics had nothing but pride to play for and the Browns made a mistake and played less than inspiring ball. The teams split the first two games, Kramer lost 4-2 and Potter won 10-5.

Sewell went with Tex Shirley in the third game of the series so that he could save Muncrief, who had thus far dominated Philadelphia, for the finale.

Since shutting out Washington on July 9th, Shirley had made just four relief appearances. His lack of work showed as he ran out of gas in the fifth inning when the Browns had a 4-0 lead. Before the inning was over he was behind 5-4 and the Browns could not catch up. The following afternoon, Muncrief blew a 3-0 lead in the seventh inning when he allowed the A's to score three runs. George Caster in his fifth inning of relief lost the game in the twelveth when George Kell hit a bases loaded drive against the rightfield wall.

The Browns were shocked in losing three of four to the lowly Athletics but luckily for them the Red Sox had only gained a game as had the Yankees. Momentarily stalled, the Tigers were in fourth place only seven games out.

ONE CHAMPIONSHIP SEASON

On their next stop in Washington, the heat, humidity and pressure of the pennant race created more friction between two teams that openly disliked each other. From the moment the Browns arrived in Washington, they had problems.

Sewell wanted Galehouse, Kramer, Stephens, McQuinn, and Christman to get a head start and a night of rest in Washington. But the hotels claimed they were booked and could not accommodate them until the whole team arrived in town. The five players slept in the hotel lobby. With a doubleheader opening the four-game series, Sewell was not happy that his players couldn't get the proper rest.

St. Louis played like tired souls as they were swept in the opening doubleheader. After losing a 2-0 lead, and the game 4-2, they were shellacked in the nightcap 12-1 as Kramer was beaten unmercifully.

The losing streak reached four and the Browns lead on second place slipped to three and a half games. In Detroit the advance ticket windows were busy taking orders for the St. Louis-Detroit series starting at the end of the week. The Browns couldn't focus on Detroit until they took care of Washington.

Jakucki momentarily got them back on track with a 5-3 win. The Browns' came from behind and won the game in the twelveth inning when Don Gutteridge hit his first home run of the season. Jakucki's complete game was only the third for St. Louis in the past fifteen.

The season finale in Griffith Stadium began as a pitchers duel until Potter was ejected for starting a brawl.

The game was scoreless when the Senators came to bat in the seventh. Three hits, an error and a sacrifice later, the Senators had three runs in and pitcher Johnny Niggeling standing on third.

George Case stepped to the plate and on the first pitch from Potter dragged a bunt down the first base line. The attempted squeeze play irked Potter who was already unhappy with letting the game get out of hand. He had words with Case as they met somewhere between home and first. Case threw a punch at Potter and both benches emptied.

When the smoke had cleared, the umpires ejected Potter, Case, and Washington's reserve infielder Eddie Butka. This brought manager Ossie Bluege out of the dugout for a lengthy argument because he thought another Brownie should have been ejected. In the fight, Case got hit a couple of times by various Browns players.

Potter, bruised nose and scratch under his eye, would be fined $100 but escaped getting his second suspension of the season.

St. Louis had two days off before playing the Tigers, but had no break from the summer heat. Sewell was frustrated with the lack of hitting and ordered everyone to take extra batting practice. The Browns were heading into Briggs Stadium with thirteen losses in their last twenty games while the three closest trailing teams were all winning in the same time span.

Gutteridge (.214), Stephens (.161), Christman (.152), and McQuinn (.136) had failed to produce with men in scoring position in the last eight games, and the pressure was landing on the shoulders of Byrnes and Zarilla who continued hitting but could not support the team like any "one" of the others was capable of.

Adding to Sewell's woes was Bob Muncrief's failure to respond to treatment for his sore arm. His last four starts were struggles (2-0, 5.38) and though he was keeping the team in the game, he was hurting himself. He had been given eight days of rest before being allowed to pitch in the first game of

Luke Sewell continued to talk about winning despite the Browns' late August slump. (National Baseball Library & Archive, Cooperstown, N.Y.)

the Sunday doubleheader. After St. Louis was shutout by Dizzy Trout, 1-0 (it was Trout's first win over the Browns after three losses), and Stubby Overmire, 5-0, in the first two games of the series, Sewell prayed he'd get a good game from his crafty righthander.

But Muncrief couldn't hold onto a 3-0 lead as the Tigers came from behind and won 5-3 behind Hal Newhouser's twenty-first win. After the game Muncrief was sent home to consult with the club surgeon about his arm. His injury was diagnosed as a strain of the muscle in his right elbow and his season was in jeopardy.

Potter salvaged the last game of the series as he held the Tigers to two runs while his teammates exploded to the tune of seventeen runs. Four hits by McQuinn, three by Kreevich and Stephens and two for Christman were enough to get the guys on a hitting streak.

The Browns were relieved to get out of Detroit still holding a three and a half game lead. Helping them were the Athletics who beat the Red Sox three out of four. Meanwhile the Yankees and Tigers moved to within four games.

The hitting continued in Cleveland as St. Louis won 8-3 behind the solid pitching of Denny Galehouse who evened his record at 6-6. And though they scored seven runs the following afternoon they lost when Caster, in his third inning of relief of Kramer, couldn't pitch out of trouble in the eighth inning. By the time Hollingsworth got the last out of the inning for Caster, the Indians had scored eight times and went home winners 12-7.

The road trip (9-13) sent the Browns into the final month looking over their shoulders. Despite the slump, many believed the Browns had the schedule on their side. After a quick six game homestand and a four game road trip, St. Louis would be home for the final sixteen games. But the Tigers - the team the Browns knew they had to watch out for - also were to play many of their final games at home while the Red Sox and Yankees had a majority of their final games against the tail-end Athletics and Senators.

But Sewell and his men couldn't worry about the others. They barely had time to lick their wounds from their visit to

Detroit as they had to get themselves together for their final four meetings with the Tigers at home.

The opener pitted Stubby Overmire (whose last appearance was a 5-0 win over the Browns) against the most consistent pitcher the Browns had, Sig Jakucki. The game was billed as a big one and played like one as both teams played scorelessly until the top of the seventh when with the aid of some poor fielding the Tigers scored two runs. An inning ending doubleplay was in progress until Stephens dropped the feed from Gutteridge. Doc Cramer followed with a single.

Down 2-0, Sewell pinch-hit Mancuso for Jakucki after Hayworth led off the bottom of the seventh inning with a single. Mancuso came through with a double to put two runners on for Gutteridge who singled, driving in two runs. Stephens singled in another to put the Browns up 3-2.

The lead didn't last long as recently called up veteran Willis Hudlin allowed the Tigers to tie the score in the eighth. The Tigers won it in the ninth when Pinky Higgins singled in Cramer. The victory went to reliever Dizzy Trout who earned his twenty-third victory. The loss clipped St. Louis' lead to two games over the Yankees who swept sinking Washington in their doubleheader.

The following afternoon Nelson Potter was gone from the game by the third inning as Newhouser stifled the Browns 6-3. The victory moved the Tigers into second place. The Browns' bullpen lost 6-3 the following afternoon when Caster and Zoldak failed to hold onto St. Louis' one run lead. Suddenly the race was up for grabs. Going into the final game of the series and the final game with the Tigers, the Browns lead was only one game over Detroit and New York and one and a half over Boston.

Kramer and the faltering Browns took the field in the finale against Dizzy Trout and quickly fell behind 1-0. Trout's great ability on the mound couldn't stop Zarilla, who after a cold week and a half with the bat, found the heat in it again with two hits and three runs batted in. Gutteridge drove in another as the Browns won 4-1 and held onto first place for another day. It was Kramer's thirteenth win of the season but first since August 12th.

The Browns hardly had time to enjoy the win when word got to the clubhouse that the Yankees had swept the Senators, moving them to within a half a game of St. Louis. The Yankees were now set to host the floundering Athletics while the Browns had to play the still competitive Indians in a doubleheader.

For the eighth time in the span of two and a half weeks, St. Louis' pitching staff failed to hold onto a lead (this time three runs) when Jakucki surrendered a three run homer to former Brownie, Roy Cullenbine. Earlier in the inning Jakucki had given up back to back run scoring doubles. The home run, which was creamed over the rightfield pavilion, marked the end of the day for the righthander. Sewell brought in Hollingsworth whose arm had been feeling pretty good the last couple of days.

One complaint about Sewell in 1943 had been that he yanked his pitchers too fast. At times during the '44 season he overcompensated in response to that criticism. With pitchers coming down with sore arms, Sewell was forced to go with his starters longer than he wanted. This translated into a worn out staff. His plight was continued when he was forced to continue with Hollingsworth, a man with arm troubles, in his fourth inning of relief work. Ken Keltner, Warren Rosar, and Mike Rocco each nailed Hollingsworth for hits and the Indians took a 6-3 lead they would not relinquish.

Potter, who had been knocked out of the box after two innings against the Tigers in his last appearance, won the nightcap 5-1. It wasn't a masterful performance; he constantly battled out of jam after jam but he made the right pitches when he needed to, causing the Indians to leave twelve men on base. It was the first of what would be six successive complete games for him in finishing the season.

In the game a riot almost ensued when Hayworth was thrown out of the game after arguing ball and strikes with home plate umpire George Pipgras. A fan threw a bottle on the field but order was restored quickly. Only a week earlier Jakucki was tossed from the game when he razzed Pipgras from the bench accusing the umpire of rooting for his old teammates, the Yankees. Pipgras was a pitcher for the Yankees for ten years. The tossing of Browns players was nothing new to Pipgras. In one game in 1938, the umpire ejected seventeen players in a Browns-White Sox game.

But while the Browns were grateful for a split, the Yankees swept the Athletics and took first place from the Browns, the first time they were out of it since May 31st. Fans in Yankee Stadium swarmed the field like they had won the World Series. The *New York Times* proclaimed the Yankees sweep of the Athletics and the subsequent move into first place as the final nail in the Browns' coffin.

Dealing with the abnormal position the Browns' were in this late in the season, some in St. Louis' press corps jumped on Sewell and Browns' management for not going to Toledo to pick up a pitcher or hitter to help with the tired men on the field. But Toledo was in a pennant race, and management elected not to weaken them. Fine play in Toledo translated into larger attendance and more money in the mother team's bank account. Barnes, Sewell, and DeWitt were confident the Browns would accomplish their bid for the pennant.

One such player on the farm was outfielder-catcher Babe Martin who hit .350 for the playoff bound Mud Hens. Fans complained that Martin should have been brought up to replace Hayworth and Mancuso but Sewell felt the pitching staff was comfortable working with the two who had been with the team since opening day. Besides, catching was not Martin's strong position. When Toledo was beaten by St. Paul in seven games Sewell called up the youngster. He got into two games getting three hits in four at bats.

The next five games in Chicago were the final games on the road for St. Louis. Now behind the Yankees, a half game out, the Browns found themselves in the strange position of seeing someone ahead of them. If there was anything positive about that position it was that the pressure to perform was now on the Yankees.

Denny Galehouse started the opener in Comiskey Park and had fallen behind 4-0 when Sewell went to Sam Zoldak. The young lefthander who had joined the team in June was doing a fine job but his inexperience worried Sewell so he had few appearances. He showed that he wasn't just sitting on the bench day-dreaming by shutting the doors on the White Sox for the next three innings. In the seventh the Browns scored two runs to get back in the game and set things up for an exciting ninth inning.

A tiring Orval Grove gave up singles to Byrnes and Zarilla before walking Stephens to load the bases. Gordon Maltzberger was brought in and he gave up a game-tying two-run single to Mike Chartak who was playing for the slumping McQuinn. It was the first of many moves that labeled Sewell a "stretch run" genius. Moore then hit a sacrifice fly to score the winning run and the Browns were back in first, tied with the Yankees. St. Louis brief return to first place was ended when Muncrief was blown out of the next game 9-5.

Kramer pitched his best game of the year the following day. After giving up a run in the first inning, Kramer shut the door on Chicago. As with each game in the series the Chicago fans, disgusted with the play of their team, stood

Vern Stephens and Don Gutteridge were top notch on the field as well as the plate. (The Bettman Archive)

and cheered everything the Browns did. They stood and cheered for thirteen innings as Kramer set the White Sox down with each passing inning. He surrendered one hit from the first to the tenth innings. Trouble was that Eddie Lopat was doing the same against the Browns. St. Louis' only run came on Kramer's second home run of the season in the eighth inning.

By the fourteenth inning Kramer had weakened. Ray Schalk singled with one out and advanced to second on Ralph Hodgin's single. After Trosky grounded out to Gutteridge to put runners on second and third, Thurman Tucker blooped the first pitch thrown to him into short rightfield. Gutteridge ran out and Byrnes ran in. The latter dived for the ball which was just out of his reach. Kramer was forced to swallow a tough 2-1 loss, dropping the Browns to third place, one game off the pace.

Potter won his fifteenth game before Jakucki pitched his second consecutive unimpressive game in the Sunday doubleheader. In frustration the latter threw the ball to the ground when Sewell walked out to the mound. Muncrief had done the same only a week earlier, causing those in the press box to think that there was dissension on the club. Sewell reassured the writers that it was just the competitiveness of both pitchers.

Detroit and New York split their doubleheaders against the Indians and Red Sox, respectively, leaving everything in the standings the way it had been the morning of the games. A quirk in the schedule had the whole league off for the next four days. The White Sox traveled with the Browns to St. Louis to continue their series there. Instead of getting some extra hitting and pitching practice in, Sewell elected to have his players rest up.

The final two weeks of the season were upon them and they were exhausted. Christman (6 HR, 77 RBI, .272) had lost 20 pounds during the season and everyone but Kreevich (6 HR, 39 RBI, .293) was suffering at the plate. Sewell found himself benching McQuinn (10 HR, 64 RBI, .254) on occasion (he had just broken an 0 for 18 slump) and Moore (5 HR, 56 RBI, .234) who after a fine June was struggling at a .207 clip the last two months. This allowed Sewell to get Mike Chartak (1 HR, 7 RBI, .235) in the lineup.

Gutteridge (1 HR, 31 RBI, .252), Stephens (17 HR, 96 RBI, .300), Byrnes (4 HR, 42 RBI, .307), and Zarilla (6 HR, 43 RBI, .298) were still playing well. Sitting on the bench was Chet Laabs (2 HR, 12 RBI, .197) who had only started eight games in the past month and a half. Hayworth (2 HR, 20 RBI, .231) and Mancuso (1 HR, 24 RBI, .210) were platooning well and surviving injury after injury while Tom

Turner (0 HR, 4 RBI, .320) filled in admirably when called on. Sewell would rely on the guys who were there since the beginning of the season and Turner didn't get into another game.

The pitching staff, which had been the glue keeping the dream together, was suffering in the last twenty-three games. Losing sixteen of those games the staff had amassed a 4.50 earned run average. This was a far cry from the 3.10 earned run average they were sporting before the slump. But they were hurting physically as well as mentally.

Hollingsworth (5-7, 4.45), who had pitched with a sore arm all year, just couldn't lift his arm anymore and would not pitch for the remainder of the regular season. Muncrief (12-7, 3.08) had suffered through a 6.69 earned run average in his last five appearances. He would make just two more appearances after it was discovered that his sore elbow was the result of bone chips. Shirley (5-4, 4.15) was suffering from the same ailment and would also make just one more appearance in the regular season. Despite the dwindling of the pitching staff Sewell went with his winners instead of risking losing the pennant with rarely used and inexperienced Sam Zoldak (0-0, 3.59) and Weldon West (0-0, 6.37), who was optioned to Oakland in the Pacific Coast League before the end of August.

In the past month, Potter (15-7, 3.12) had come through with some great games but Kramer (13-13, 2.69), Jakucki (10-9, 3.95) and Galehouse (7-8, 3.35) were struggling despite occasional flashes of brilliance. Sewell was beginning to use Jakucki more in relief to spell Caster (6-6, 2.42, 7 saves) who, with exception of one game against Cleveland, when he gave up nine runs in three innings, was showing no signs of slowing up.

The Browns were slipping and this worried many of their fans. But they had a date with destiny and Chet Laabs was the chaperon.

ONE CHAMPIONSHIP SEASON

September 14, 1944

	WON	LOST	GB
New York Yankees	76	61	—
Detroit Tigers	75	61	½
St. Louis Browns	75	63	1½
Boston Red Sox	73	64	3
Cleveland Indians	65	72	11
Philadelphia Athletics	64	75	13
Chicago White Sox	63	74	13
Washington Senators	58	80	18½

CHAPTER 9

The Wait Is Over
(September 15 - October 1)

"I'd rather have our job in the last four days against Washington than the Browns' task of facing the Yankees."

— Steven O'Neill
(Tigers mgr.)

For four days of inactivity, the American League's injured players tried to heal their wounds and catch their breath for the homestretch.

The train ride home from Chicago, though short, was hard to deal with as the whole midwest seemed to be going through a heat wave. Because air conditioning was just coming into being the team was forced to pick up blocks of ice and do as they did in Sportsman's Park's dugout, placing fans behind them to cool off the car.

They met at Sportsman's Park on Friday morning, September 15th. Coaches Freddy Hofmann and Zach Taylor worked with the pitchers in the bullpen that lay just beyond the leftfield foul line, and Sewell sat in the corner of the shaded dugout watching a given batting and fielding practice. Most of the players worked shirtless as the summer heat had yet to leave Missouri.

Sewell was mulling over his outfield situation and had a hunch. He knew he wanted Byrnes (.341 the past month and a half) and Kreevich (.313 during the same span) in rightfield and centerfield, respectively, but in leftfield he had either the slumping Gene Moore (.203 over the past two and a half months), the hot Al Zarilla (.400 in his last seven games), or Laabs who was hitting only .197.

His initial thought was to play Zarilla, but Laabs was stinging the ball in batting practice. Sewell was impressed with Laabs' swinging but played Zarilla in the first game of the Chicago series.

With everyone as rested as they could be, Sewell elected to go with Denny Galehouse in the opener. Galehouse was not exactly pitching great ball lately. His last three appearances netted him two losses and a 6.14 earned run average. Still, Sewell went with his hunches and set the rotation for the rest of the season as Galehouse, Kramer, Potter, and Muncrief. Because of Jakucki's ineffectiveness of late, he would be helping Caster in the bullpen.

As the Browns prepared themselves for the opening of the homestand, a radio report from St. Louis sports commentator Bill Stern accused the team of being involved in the biggest scandal since the 1919 "Black Sox." The story was to appear the following day in *Collyer's Eye and Baseball World*. The writer never detailed his accusation during the radio report but did hint that baseball's hierarchy wanted the Browns to slow down and let another club win the pennant so that more money could be made on the series.

Barnes laughed at the notion that the players and the organization would pass up a chance at their first ever pennant and explained to the *St. Louis Post Dispatch* that Stern had written to him some time ago demanding to know why the Browns were slumping so severely. Barnes dismissed the letter and felt that this radio report and article were just a way for the writer to get back at him. Only four days later the report was repudiated by Stern and forgotten.

The report may have been the stimulus the Browns needed for the stretch run. Again the hands of fate were on the side of St. Louis when in the first inning the White Sox had scored a run. But Sewell walked out to the plate and informed the umpire that Ed Carnett had batted out of turn and was thus out. Thus the inning ending without a run. The Browns scored two in the first and never looked back as Galehouse pitched a great game and won 5-1.

Kramer threw a one-hitter the next day as St. Louis drubbed Chicago 9-0. Coupled with New York's loss to Philadelphia the Browns were back in first, a half game up on Detroit and New York.

Potter handled Chicago in the first game of the double-header 5-1 but when Muncrief got no relief help from Zoldak and Jakucki in the 8-2 nightcap loss, the Browns again fell from first place. This time it was the Tigers who moved into the lead position when they swept the Indians and the Yankees lost twice to the Athletics.

After a day off the Senators were in town and the bad blood between the two teams again showed itself in the first game of the series.

In a game won by the Senators 6-0 (all six runs scoring in the eleventh inning) Washington knuckleballer Roger Wolff threw a fastball and hit Stephens with a pitch. Stephens shook it off and trotted down to first after nearly charging the mound. But Sewell, perhaps more angered over the six-run eleventh inning, grabbed a bat from the rack and walked out onto the playing field were he was promptly intercepted by the umpire.

Sewell waved the bat in the air while calling Wolff every foul name in the book. Eventually order was restored but not before Stephens had a few things to say while standing on first. The incident didn't do anything to fuel the team for the rest of the inning but it did inspire them for the rest of the season.

The Browns won the following afternoon 5-2. Kramer got his fifteenth win in a relatively peaceful game. Laabs went three for four with two runs batted in. After the game Sewell informed him that he was the starting leftfielder for the last twelve days of the season.

The next day's game being the last meeting of the two teams for the season, trouble began before the first pitch was thrown.

The Senators were on the field taking batting practice as Brownie catcher Tom Turner sat in the dugout. While watching the grey flanneled visitors take their swings, Turner began hurling expletives. This didn't sit well with Cuban-born Roberto Ortiz.

Ortiz took his last swing and walked over to the Browns' dugout. Still holding his Louisville Slugger he suggested Turner come out and settle the score. Turner would oblige but only if they fought with their hands.

Ortiz tossed the bat to the side as a group of players began to make a circle around the two men. Just before a punch could be thrown, a fan leapt from the stands and pleaded with the fighting players to come to their senses. Ellis Clary, known as an instigator and fighter, stepped in front of the man and threatened to punch him out if he didn't butt out. The man preferred his facial features in the present condition and backed off as Ortiz and Turner rolled on the ground, getting their share of punching in. When enough was enough, the players were pulled apart. Turner was dazed while Ortiz damaged his thumb on Turner's face.

In the game, Nelson Potter and the Browns crushed Washington 9-4, ending their visitations with one another. The Browns were still a game and a half behind the Tigers with ten games to play.

After taking the first two games of their series with Philadelphia, running their winning streak to five games, the Browns won yet another game typical of a team of destiny. Kramer had pitched his heart out in front of 12,000 fans and looked to be robbed of his sixteenth win when the Browns came to bat in the bottom of the ninth down by the score of 2-0.

After Laabs flied out, Stephens lined a single to leftfield. He was erased when Byrnes grounded into a force play so the Browns were down to their last out. McQuinn worked the count to three and two before walking so the Browns now had the tying run on first base.

Sewell sent Shirley in to run for McQuinn in hopes that if Christman could drive one in the gap, the game could be won. Christman wasted no time, driving Jess Flores' first pitch into left centerfield for an extra base hit. Byrnes scored easily but as Shirley rounded third he stumbled, falling to his knees ten feet short of home plate. He scrambled in a crawl towards the plate and luckily, the throw by shortstop Edgar Busch was wild. Shirley scored to tie the game and Christman took third on the bad throw.

Joe Berry was brought in to end the threat and so it seemed as he got Baker to hit an easy fly to center. But Philadelphia's Bobby Estalella dropped the ball and Christman came in to score. The win moved the Browns to within a half a game of the Tigers who had lost to Philadelphia.

St. Louis won the first two games against Boston to increase their winning streak to seven, tying them with Detroit for first place. Both games were gutty performances, Potter and Jakucki, each shutting out the Red Sox, 3-0 and 1-0 respectively. The start of Jakucki came about when it was learned that Muncrief's arm needed rest or his career would be in jeopardy. Muncrief sat out the rest of the regular season.

The final game of series looked in doubt as rain fell on the midwest all night and day. It was four o'clock when the scoreboard noted the Tigers had beaten the Athletics despite the rain in Detroit. This momentarily put the Browns a half game back. Because of the travel restrictions this game could not be made up, no matter what the outcome was at season's end.

The Sox had a six o'clock train to Chicago but agreed to postpone it for an early morning trip so that the Browns could play. They had to ask permission from the league and they got it. One stipulation was that no inning could begin after 11:05 P.M. and the game would be forced to end at 11:20 regardless of the score or inning.

With it still raining, the game was played. The field was muddy and everyone was soaked. The wait for the game got on the Browns' players nerves and it showed during the game as they lost 4-1. It looked like their pennant hopes were dashed because the Tigers defeated the Athletics 4-0, setting the Browns back by one game with four games to play.

Everyone in the league was rained out on the 28th so the Friday schedules were filled with doubleheaders. If Detroit won both games against the Senators or the Yankees won against the Browns, St. Louis' season would be over. The Tigers had already beaten Washington fifteen of eighteen times during the season and the Browns had lost ten of eighteen to the Yankees.

Many of the Browns' players and Sewell would later in their lives say that they reached their peak as a team during this final series.

Kramer pitched in the first game of the doubleheader, who after a shaky August was pitching his best baseball in the month that it counted most. In September his record was 4-1 with a 1.28 earned run, his only loss coming in thirteen innings against the White Sox. The Yankees had twelve-game winner Ernie Bonham going. Johnny Lindell singled home Snuffy Stirnweiss but, from that point on, Kramer was in control of the game while St. Louis' bats rallied.

In the third Kramer lifted a fly ball to deep centerfield. Lindell misjudged it and it fell for a double. Gutteridge bunted for an infield hit before Kreevich and Laabs singled in runs.

The score remained 2-1 until the eighth inning when struggling George McQuinn hit his eleventh home run of the season, sealing the Browns' 4-1 win. It also eliminated the Yankees from the race because, as the huge scoreboard in Sportsman's Park showed, Detroit had won their opener.

The news wasn't only bad for New York, but for the Browns. Going in the nightcap for Detroit was twenty-seven game winner Steve Trout. The Tigers looked to be a cinch for clinching a tie. But Potter, who had pitched five consecutive complete games, couldn't worry about what Detroit was going to do. He confidently took the mound against seventeen-game winner Hank Borowy.

The Yankee ace pitched a masterful game, allowing the Browns just two hits. Gutteridge started the game with a double and moved to third on a wild pitch. Kreevich then grounded to second as Gutteridge scored. Borowy would allow three more baserunners (two walks and a hit) but his teammates were just as baffled by Potter.

The Yankees were unable to mount any kind of rally until the eighth inning. With the score still 1-0 and one out, Stirnweiss and Russ Derry singled. After Hersh Martin popped out, Lindell came to the plate.

Potter tried to put something extra on the ball but Lindell drilled the pitch into centerfield. Kreevich started running in for the ball before realizing it was going to sail over his head. He ran back as hard as he could, backpeddling on the wet grass before turning to catch the ball over his right shoulder. The rally was over but the Yankees had one more shot.

The 6,000 fans who showed to Sportsman's Park that day were as loud as they could be when the Browns took the field in the ninth. The scoreboard had showed the Senators enjoying a 9-2 lead. A win for St. Louis would tie them for first with two games left.

Nick Etten was on second with two out when future Hall of Famer Paul Waner came to the plate. Waner barely got a piece of the pitch and blooped one over second base. But Gutteridge ran back and leaped high in the air, snagging the batted ball. With the final zero tacked on the Detroit linescore, the Browns fans were jubilant. Their once hapless Brownies were tied for first place with two games left.

While Newhouser was winning his twenty-ninth game the following afternoon, 7-3, Galehouse pitched the game of his career in front of 17,000 fans. With the aid of a home run by Gene Moore (his first start in three weeks) Galehouse five hit the Yankees, 2-0, and sent the season into the final day in a tie. The prospects of the first playoff game ever was staring St. Louis and Detroit in the face.

The Wait Is Over

Detroit may have thought a tie on the last day was not all together a bad thing because they had won the coin toss that decided where a one-game playoff would be played. The fact that it would be in Detroit, where the Browns had lost five of their last six, added to their confidence.

Although it was the first of October, St. Louis still could not shake the heat and humidity of the summer. As the thermometer peaked in the upper eighties, the Browns took batting practice and the fans filed in with much enthusiasm. And they filed in by the thousands as over 34,000 crammed into sold out Sportsman's Park. Lines formed for general admission seats as early as seven in the morning. An hour before the game the streets were packed.

Browns' fielders shagged flyballs and instinctively kept one eye on the huge scoreboard that rested beyond the left field seats. As the fans groped for their seats and cold soda, they too kept an eye on the scoreboard. Because of the one hour time differential, the Tiger-Senator game was already in progress.

Everyone in the park knew that the Senators were pitching Dutch Leonard against Steve Trout, who had only one day of rest. But unbeknownest to everyone was that Leonard had received a phone call before the game telling him he could make a lot of money if he lost the game on purpose. He informed Washington management of the call and they told him to just go out and beat Detroit. But, fearing violence he pitched under added pressure.

The Browns, with the possibility of their first ever pennant looming in front of them, were surprisingly loose as game time approached. With the game's first pitch the Browns bench was alive, teammates cheered each other on until hoarse. If there was any nervousness felt by the team, it concerned their starting pitcher Sig Jakucki.

Only the night before, the team as a whole begged the pitcher, who was known to have a few drinks, not to indulge in the bottled spirits. He reluctantly agreed and showed up at the park on game day as sober as a new born baby. A lot of the players were relieved but rumors are that after his pregame rubdown he had a couple of shots.

With twenty-five minutes to go before game time the players chatted about their hopes while keeping an eye on the scoreboard. "Goose eggs" stared out from the Detroit-Washington linescore until the top of the fourth inning when a "3" was placed on the spot that belonged to the Senators. The packed house burst into wild applause.

Chet Laabs was taking a breather on the bench. Sewell had penciled him in the lineup in the third slot as he had for the past two weeks. In that span the leftfielder was hitting .340 with seven runs batted in. Despite the impressive statistics, no one knew what kind of day he would have.

By the time the game began, the Browns looked pre-occupied with the scoreboard and very uneasy on the field. With two out, Hersh Martin tripled and then scored when Johnny Lindell hit a grounder in the hole that Stephens fielded but threw away.

In the third, Christman bobbled a roller hit by Snuffy Stirnweiss who then stole second. He would take third when Hayworth threw the ball into centerfield for St. Louis' third error in three innings. Martin then hit a shot off the right-field screen for a double and the Yankees were up 2-0.

The game went into the bottom of the fourth and the St. Louis crowd, which had thus far been quiet, began cheering for a rally. The Tigers were losing 4-0 going into the bottom of the ninth inning and the crowd could smell a pennant. Problem was the Browns didn't look like they could smell it until Kreevich led off with a single.

Chet Labbs hits two of the most important home runs in his career and the Browns' history. (UPI/Bettman)

Up to the plate stepped Laabs who took the second pitch deep into the left-centerfield stands, almost beyond the back wall, to tie the score at 2-2. As he rounded the bases the scoreboard showed that Washington had beaten Detroit 4-1 so now the fate of St. Louis rested in their own hands.

The Browns followed the homer by loading the bases with one out but Christman and Hayworth couldn't bring anyone in. The rally fell short, but set the stage for the next inning.

After Mel Queen got Jakucki and Gutteridge on outs, Kreevich singled. Queen did not want the same results as the inning before and pitched carefully to Laabs, running the count to three and one.

ONE CHAMPIONSHIP SEASON

Laabs dug his right foot deep into the batter's box and sent the next offering in almost the same spot as the inning before for his second homer of the game. The Browns were on top 4-2. The crowd disregarding the heat and humidity was whipped into a frenzy. The foundations of Sportsman's Park were literally shaking. Stephens capped off the scoring with his twentieth home run over the rightfield pavilion in the eighth inning.

Sewell left the ball in Jakucki's hand in the ninth inning. Though he was baking under the weight of his uniform (the liquor had probably seeped out of his pours) the adrenalin from the crowd was enough to shake off the fatigue. Still, Sewell had Muncrief throwing in the bullpen. Jakucki retired Lindell on a long drive to right-center which Moore hauled in before Etten singled past Gutteridge. Crosetti then flied out and Oscar Grimes stepped to the plate at 3:37 P.M.

Grimes popped the first pitch up. McQuinn circled under it in foul territory and snagged the ball in his mitt. The crowd, which had fallen silent as the ball descended, burst into loud applause as McQuinn jumped in the air.

The crowd cheered and cheered while the team made its way into the dugout. Torn newspaper and programs were fluttering through the air. There was no flooding the field by fans trying to grab hats from players or even to pat them on the back. They, like their team, were exhausted. They had fought a tough battle all the way to the end.

The city rejoiced through the night with an occasional auto parade cut short by policemen threatening their drivers with loss of gas rationing coupons. But the taverns were alive till the wee hours of the morning.

The Browns had lost seventeen of twenty-five games from late August to early September. During that slump they had blown a seven game lead and were even accused of los-

Donald Barnes is surrounded by his players after the Browns won their first ever pennant. Winning pitcher Sig Jakucki is shirtless. (Missouri Historical Society/Sports 7)

ing purposely, but they showed true grit and determination. While a lesser team might have choked, St. Louis battled to the end, fortified by a streak that saw them win fourteen of their last seventeen games.

The hitting of Vern Stephens (20 HR, 109 RBI, .293), Milt Byrnes (4 HR, 45 RBI, .295), Mark Christman (6 HR, 83 RBI, .271), and Mike Kreevich (5 HR, 44 RBI, .301) never let up. Coming off the bench Al Zarilla (6 HR, 45 RBI, .299) proved a valuable asset. George McQuinn (11 HR, 72 RBI, .250), Don Gutteridge (3 HR, 36 RBI, .245), and Gene Moore (6 HR, 58 RBI, .238) all reflected their fatigue by season's end but none ever showed any signs of giving up.

ONE CHAMPIONSHIP SEASON

When the season began the weak link in the team was the catching but by season's end Red Hayworth (1 HR, 25 RBI, .222) and Frank Mancuso (1 HR, 24 RBI, .205) were just as important as coaches Fred Hofmann and Zach Taylor in molding the pitching staff.

The pitching staff literally won it all in the final ten games by surrendering a total of only twelve runs. Nelson Potter (19-7, 2.83), Jack Kramer (17-13, 2.49), and Sig Jakucki (13-9, 3.55) together won eleven games down the stretch without a loss to give the Browns their first pennant.

Bob Muncrief (13-8, 3.08), Al Hollingsworth (5-7, 4.45), and Tex Shirley (5-4, 4.16) were unable to pitch effectively down the stretch because of their injuries, but Sewell was confident they would be better for the World Series.

Denny Galehouse (9-10, 3.12) also pitched effectively with three complete games. Because of the excellence of the starting rotation, George Caster (6-6, 2.44, 12 saves) was able to rest up for much of September after being overworked during July and August.

The Browns headed down the tunnel towards a clubhouse that was filled with Falstaff Beer and Coca Cola bottles. Donald Barnes was shedding tears of happiness as he hugged each member of the team. He wore a large size button on his jacket with the Browns' emblem of the knight on a horse in triumphant gallop. The Browns had finally lived up to an emblem that signified the dreams of their fans.

FINAL STANDINGS

	Won	Lost	GB
St. Louis Browns	89	65	—
Detroit Tigers	88	66	1
New York Yankees	83	71	6
Boston Red Sox	77	77	12
Cleveland Indians	72	82	17
Philadelphia Athletics	72	82	17
Chicago White Sox	71	83	18
Washington Senators	64	90	25

ONE CHAMPIONSHIP SEASON

CHAPTER 10

The Streetcar Series

"We'll take the Cardinals in four straight."

— Milt Byrnes

The streets surrounding Sportsman's Park were abuzz with excitement. The expensive reserved seats which were sold by two's for $37.50, (a price hike because of a hike in federal taxes) were being sold by scalpers (yes, there were scalpers in 1944) for $150.

While the rest of the league worried that an all-St. Louis series would be a financial failure, the Department of Transportation was hoping for such a meeting. If Detroit, Boston, or New York had won, the series would not have followed the 2-32 format we know today. Instead, the first three games would have been scheduled in St. Louis and the last four in the American League city. This no doubt would have been an edge for the American League club. As far as this series was concerned, the Browns were the home team for games three, four, and five.

ONE CHAMPIONSHIP SEASON

The Department of Transportation also influenced the sale of tickets in that the Browns and Cardinals had to offer most of the tickets to St. Louis residents instead of the usual cross country offerings. This ruling delighted the fine people of St. Louis.

Browns management still allowed servicemen to watch the game for no charge, but the kids "Brown's Brigade" cards were not accepted. Most understood and hunched around radios to hear the game.

The crowds which came to watch the Series split their allegiance down the middle. For the most part, the young fans rooted for the Cardinals who were consistent winners in their young memories, and the older fans, remembering the days of the great but pennantless Browns, rooted for their children's rivals. There were times though that one team had more fans than the other in attendance.

Being in the Series was not only new for the Browns' fans but for all of the team's players. Not one Browns player had ever appeared in a World Series game. Only the coaching staff had that privilege, all three having appeared as catchers.

This was the fourth Series for Fred Hofmann, who caught a game for the 1923 Yankees; the third Series for Zach Taylor, who caught a game for the 1929 Cubs; and the second Series for Luke Sewell, who caught one game for the 1933 Indians.

So everyone on the team was understandably nervous as they glanced upon the empty grandstands of Sportsman's Park the morning of the first game.

Adding to their nervousness was the fact that the Cardinals were appearing in their third consecutive World Series and a few of their players had already experienced the crazed excitement that accompanies it.

The Cardinals were coming off a season in which they won the pennant by fourteen and a half games over second place Pittsburgh. They had won 73 of their first 100 games, spending only four days out of first place. Their 105 wins marked the third consecutive season they reached the century mark in wins.

The Cardinals had a potent lineup. Their outfield of Stan Musial (12 HR, 94 RBI, .347), Johnny Hopp (11 HR, 72 RBI, .336), and Danny Litwhiler (15 HR, 82 RBI, .264) packed punch and aggressiveness. The infield of Ray Sanders (12 HR, 102 RBI, .295), Emil Verban (0 HR, 43 RBI, .257), MVP Marty Marion (6 HR, 63 RBI, .267), and Whitey Kurowski (20 HR, 87 RBI, .270) led the league in fewest errors. Behind the plate was the great Walker Cooper (13 HR, 72 RBI, .317). The Cardinals led the league in hits, doubles, home runs, runs scored, batting average, and slugging percentage.

The beneficiary of this hitting and fielding was the pitching staff who boasted the league's best earned run average with the likes of Mort Cooper (22-7, 2.46), Ted Wilks (17-4, 2.64), Max Lanier (17-12, 2.65), Harry Brecheen (16-5, 2.86), and Blix Donnelly (2-1, 2.13).

But going into the Series the Cardinals were hurting. Lanier had a bad back, had lost seven consecutive games, and hadn't pitched since September 22nd. Musial was suffering from a knee injury. Marion was sick, and reliever Al Jurisich had a bad arm. Still, manager Billy Southworth had enough talent to compete and, not surprisingly, the Cardinals were predicted to dispatch of the Browns in five easy games.

On the field players from both teams loosened up on their respective sidelines as they focused on the 2 P.M. Central War Time starting time. It was a cool afternoon with highs in the lower seventies. There was the threat of rain but it did not materialize.

ONE CHAMPIONSHIP SEASON

Knowing how dominating the Cardinals appeared to be, Sewell, trying to get every advantage that he could, refused to name his starting pitcher until the day of the game. The only one to know was Denny Galehouse who was told during the final game of the season. Sworn to secrecy, Galehouse didn't disappoint his manager. The choice of Galehouse did not sit well with fans or the press. While many pointed to Potter, Sewell went with his hunch. His hunches had been working for a month so he wasn't about to let anyone influence his decision.

In order to get more people into the park the centerfield bleachers were opened up. Many fans would be wearing light colored shirts which made for a bad background for the hitters. Fastball pitchers like Mort Cooper, Max Lanier, and Galehouse would benefit from this distraction. The pitchers used this advantage to dominate the Series.

The crowd was relatively quiet while the players took batting practice but as soon as the Cardinals took the field, the adrenaline in the players was the same as the one in the fans.

Cooper, a World Series veteran, showed his experience during the first three innings on the mound. Galehouse on the other hand was nervous and proved it when he surrendered five hits in the first three innings. The Cardinals loaded the bases in the third with one out but Galehouse bore down, struckout Whitey Kurowski, and got Dan Litwhiler to ground out.

The Browns struck first when with two out in the fourth inning Gene Moore stood at the plate. He chocked up on the bat after two strikes were thrown by him. He jumped on the third pitch and singled to rightfield. George McQuinn came to the plate and after looking at one pitch promptly smashed the next offering of Cooper's just beyond the screen

Don Gutteridge strikes out in Game 1.
(The Bettman Archive)

of the right field pavilion. It was the first series homer by a
St. Louis Brown. It was also the last.

The crowd erupted in applause as McQuinn circled the
bases. A smile on his face could be seen from the farthest
seat in the house. The ovation lasted two minutes as
McQuinn was greeted in the dugout by his back-slapping
teammates.

Galehouse settled down after his early inning nervousness
and allowed only one more hit until the ninth inning when
Marty Marion doubled to lead off the inning. He eventually
scored on a sacrifice fly but the Cardinals could do no more
and the Browns took their first ever World Series game, 2-1.

Before the second game, Benny Rader and his 25-piece
band blared out their rendition of "Milkman Keep Those

Bottles Quiet" while both teams tossed the ball around and the grounds crew threw dry sand on the wet infield. Many a fan was wet, the rains during the night having soaked those who waited in line for good tickets. The tavern across the street was filled with fans arguing over who had the better team, but it emptied out when the Dodier street gates opened at 10 A.M. with the sun shining brightly on the park.

The Browns had their chances to win this game. Take away any of their misplays and they would have been up two games to none. A couple of Brown errors led to Cardinal runs in the third and fourth innings.

The first damaging error came in the third inning after Emil Verban singled to leftfield. Max Lanier then attempted to bunt the runner over. His bunt was not a good one. It hung in the air long enough for Potter to catch it on the fly. Verban had clung to first base because he too thought it was catchable. But the ball fell to the ground and was fumbled by Potter. He then hurriedly threw the ball wide of first. Gutteridge who was covering the bag tried to keep one foot on the bag and reach for the ball but he wasn't tall enough and the ball strayed into rightfield. Laabs retrieved the ball and held Verban at third base. Johnny Hopp then grounded to Gutteridge at second as Verban came in to score the first run of the game.

In the fourth inning with one out, Potter walked Ray Sanders. Kurowski singled to put runners on first and second for Marty Marion. Marion's grounder to Christman looked like an inning ending doubleplay, but the ball bounced off his mitt and the bases were loaded. Potter was able to keep the scoring to a Verban sacrifice fly, but it looked like the Cardinals already had enough runs because Lanier was tossing a great game.

Al Zarilla slides safely into third base as Whitey Kurowski awaits the late throw. (The Bettman Archive)

The Browns were held to one hit through the first six innings when they attempted to break up Lanier's rhythm. He showed no signs of being disturbed when he set down the first two Browns (McQuinn struckout and Christman popped out) in the seventh inning.

But Moore, who aside from McQuinn was the only one hitting, singled to centerfield. Hayworth followed with a one hop shot off the leftfield wall for a run scoring double. Sewell went for the tie and sent Mancuso up to pinch hit for Potter. Mancuso had only one pinch at bat during the season, but Sewell had another one of his hunches. Mancuso proceeded to boost the "genius" label Sewell was getting as he singled to center to tie the score.

It looked like the Browns were going to put the game away in the eighth inning, in what may have been the turning point of the series, when Kreevich led off with a double. Billy Southworth came out to the mound and called on Blix Donnelly to get the Cardinals out of the inning. With Laabs, Stephens, and McQuinn due up, his work was cut out for him. Laabs failed in his attempt to bunt the runner over and eventually struckout. Stephens was badly fooled on a changeup and also struckout. Donnelly elected to intentionally walk McQuinn giving Christman a shot at winning the game. Donnelly's side arm motion had Christman flailing at each pitch and he struckout, ending the Browns' golden opportunity. Donnelly would strikeout six of the ten players he faced in his relief appearance.

With Donnelly still on the mound in the eleventh, McQuinn led off with a drive to deep right-centerfield. The ball hit the top of the screen, missing going into the stands by inches, and fell to the field. It was picked up and thrown back in time to halt McQuinn at second.

Christman then came to the plate and bunted down the third base line. It looked like a perfect bunt as it hugged the grass. Donnelly flew off the mound, scooped up the ball, and whirling around threw a strike to Kurowski at third base. McQuinn was tagged out and another Browns rally was stifled.

With Muncrief pitching his fourth inning of relief, the Cardinals mounted their winning rally in the bottom half of the eleventh. Ken O'Dea's pinch singling brought in the winning run and the Cardinals tied the series.

There was no day off between the second and third games but the privilege of being the home team was switched to the Browns. The series was tied at a game apiece but it very easily could have been a two games to none edge for the Browns. Worrying Sewell was the non-existent hitting of his sluggers Laabs and Stephens as well as his slap hitters in Gutteridge and Christman. All were hitless in eight at bats after the first two games.

Senator Harry S. Truman attended Game Three while members from both teams crowded around him for photos. Before the game many of the fans booed the Browns as they took batting practice. There was plenty of red seen in the stands as Zach Taylor (who was tossing batting practice) stood on the mound waving his arms in the air for the fans to get louder. The crowd obliged but only after Tom Turner hit a few into the bleachers. Jack Kramer was warming up in the bullpen and was feeling good. Unfortunately poor fielding would put him and his team in a hole again.

With one out, Hopp grounded to Stephens who let the ball roll between his legs. Hopp stretched it into second and Stan Musial stepped to the plate. Kramer made a great pitch to the future Hall of Famer, forcing him to popout to Stephens who drew mock applause. Kramer still had to get past Walker Cooper. He was overmatched as Cooper lined a single into left-centerfield to put the Cardinals up 1-0.

Seventeen-game winning rookie Ted Wilks was on the mound for the Cardinals and he seemed nervous with all the World Series attention. In the second inning he got out of trouble after walking three batters.

Noticing Wilks' uneasiness on the mound, the Browns went after everything he threw and broke through in the third inning when with two out Moore and Stephens singled back to back. McQuinn continued his hot hitting by singling to centerfield scoring Moore to tie the game. Zarilla, getting the start in leftfield, then singled to leftfield to bring home Stephens. Christman then lined a pitch up the middle and the Browns had a 3-1 lead. When Hopp threw to the plate in an attempt to get McQuinn the runners took an extra base. The Browns now had runners on second and third.

ONE CHAMPIONSHIP SEASON

Southworth came out to talk to Ted Wilks and ordered him to intentionally walk Hayworth so that there would be a force at any base with the pitcher coming up. Kramer, who had two home runs during the season, must have looked menacing at the plate because Wilks' first pitch bounced in the dirt and past Cooper, allowing Zarilla to score from third. Southworth came back out and yanked his rookie pitcher in favor of Fred Schmidt who retired Kramer on a groundout.

Kramer was in control the rest of the way except for allowing another unearned run in the seventh. With one out and Sanders on first, Kurowski grounded to Stephens. The shortstop flipped the ball to Gutteridge for one out but the second baseman threw the ball wild to first and Kurowski took second. Marion singled to score a run but Kramer prevented further damage. The Browns scored two in their half of the seventh on a wild pitch and a third hit of the game from McQuinn.

Kramer began to tire in the eighth when he allowed three consecutive hard hit balls. Fortunately one of them was an out. Moore had raced back to the wall in rightfield to snare a line drive by Musial.

The Cardinals had runners on second and third when Sewell walked out to the mound. Kramer didn't want to leave but Sewell knew he had Hollingsworth ready in the pen. Hayworth assured the manager that Kramer was still throwing fine. For the first time in a long time Sewell elected not to go with his hunch. He went back to the dugout and sat in his usual corner.

Kramer then fanned Sanders before getting Kurowski to fly out to Moore. The Cardinals did not threaten in the ninth inning, and the Browns took Game Three, 6-2. They were now up two games to one and looked in good shape with Sig Jakucki scheduled to take the mound the following day.

George Caster signs autographs before getting set for the fourth game of the series. (AP/Wide World Photo)

Sewell was concerned with his team's fielding. Six errors by the otherwise fine fielding Browns had translated into four unearned runs of the six allowed by the pitching staff. Take away half those errors and the Cardinals may have been looking at elimination. As a team they were only hitting .170.

It was a sunny afternoon as Game Four of the series got underway. There were more white shirts in centerfield than usual but that wasn't what Laabs was complaining about when he came to bat in the second inning. He was bothered by a reflecting light which Umpire George Pipgras failed to notice. When Sewell and Southworth both walked out to the mound to confer with the umpire they *noticed* that two brass buttons on the hats of two servicemen sitting in the bleachers was the cause of the distraction. They obligingly removed their hats to the amusement of their fellow bleacherites.

On the field Jakucki wasn't in the best of shape. His love of the bottle was not the problem in this case though. The morning after he pitched his great game against the Yankees on the final day of the regular season, Jakucki woke up with an abcessed tooth. The tooth bothered him all week despite the remedies used to control the pain. He had the option of pulling the tooth but worried that the after affects would hurt his pitching.

From the first inning it was evident that Jakucki was having trouble finding the plate. The first two pitches of the game were way out of the strike zone though he finally struckout Litwhiler with a pitch in the dirt. But Hopp followed with a grounder up the middle that Gutteridge could only knock down. Musial then hit a crushing blow over the rightfield pavilion. In the third he allowed two more runs to score before finally leaving for a pinch hitter in the bottom of the third inning.

Meanwhile the Browns were being shut down by Harry Brecheen. The Browns had a hit in each of the first six innings but were unable to push a run across.

In the first inning with Kreevich on first, Moore drove a pitch deep into right-centerfield. Hopp ran back and snared the ball making one of the better World Series plays. One potential rally gone. In the second inning Laabs flied out deep to Litwhiler before McQuinn and Christman singled. But Hayworth grounded into a doubleplay, ending another potential rally. In the next three innings the Browns stranded Gutteridge twice and Laabs, who recorded his first hit of the series.

Hollingsworth had pitched fine relief for four innings, allowing just one run before Tex Shirley shut down the Cardinals in the final two innings. But the Browns could only scratch out one run in the eighth inning when Moore lead off with a walk and moved to third on Stephens' single off the rightfield screen. Laabs then drilled a pitch up the middle but Marion snared it and flipped it to Verban who turned and threw it to Sanders to double up Laabs. Moore scored but the big inning was over.

The series was now even as Game One winner Denny Galehouse was set to oppose Game One loser Mort Cooper. Only a seventh game could be more important than a tied series going into the fifth game.

The excitement of the series was reaching a fever pitch in the stands. Every game had been sold out, with standing room only in the fifth game. Concessions were going wild as Sportsman's Park had sold more hot dogs, peanuts, soda, and beer than in the previous two World Series put together. Before the fifth game concessionaire Blake Harper had to fire a dozen vendors for selling goods for five cents more than what they were supposed to sell for. Scalping wasn't reserved for seating.

The expected pitching duel between Cooper and Galehouse was realized. There were twenty-two strikeouts in the game, a record at the time, as Cooper recorded twelve of them. While Cooper was ahead in strikeouts Galehouse was running beside him in scoreless innings until the sixth.

Galehouse made two bad pitches in the whole game. In the sixth inning Sanders hit a three-one pitch over the rightfield pavilion to give the Cardinals a 1-0 lead. Then in the eighth Litwhiler hit the first pitch into the right-centerfield bleachers (just missing the rightfield screen) to put the Cardinals up 2-0.

ONE CHAMPIONSHIP SEASON

The only time the Browns made any kind of noise was in the sixth when Kreevich led off with a single. Moore attempted to bunt him over but the bunt was hard enough that Cooper was able to throw to second and get the force. That proved important because Stephens followed with a single to center sending Moore to third instead of tying the game. McQuinn then walked (loading the bases) and that brought manager Southworth out to the mound.

After a lenghthy conference Southworth left his star pitcher in the game. Cooper proceeded to strikeout Zarilla looking and Christman swinging. The Browns never got anything going in the final three innings as Cooper confused the Brownie batters by throwing hard stuff instead of his usual slow curve and fork ball. In desperation Sewell sent three pinch hitters to the plate in the ninth. Milt Byrnes and Chet Laabs were struckout looking, followed by Mike Chartak's wild swing at strike three.

The Cardinals were back to being the home team for Game Six. The Browns had their backs to the wall, new to them as the final series of the season with the Yankees attested. Their fate for the afternoon was in the hands of nineteen game winner Nelson Potter. If he could get a win then Kramer would be set for Game Seven.

After a relatively warm weathered series, the temperatures dropped. With the thermometer barely getting to fifty degrees, fans were bundled in blankets and overcoats. Coffee was the drink of choice but it wasn't the caffeine that got the adrenaline going. The fans were alive with every pitch and many rooted for the underdog Browns to take the series to seven games.

The Browns did the best they could, drawing first blood. In the top of the second after Stephens had struckout, Laabs drove a pitch into deep centerfield. The ball bounced off the 425 foot sign and was retrieved by Hopp. Laabs cruised into

*Mike Kreevich is forced out at second by Marty Marion in a failed
sacrifice attempt by Gene Moore. (The Bettman Archive)*

third with a triple. McQuinn followed with a single to drive
in Laabs and the Browns had a 1-0 lead.

Potter was in control until the fourth inning when he
was the victim of yet another error from the infield. Musial
led off with a flyout before Cooper walked. Sanders followed
with a single to rightfield sending Cooper to third. Kurowski
hit a grounder to Stephens with doubleplay written all over
it, but Stephens' throw to Gutteridge pulled him off the bag

and all hands were safe. Cooper scored on the play tying the game. The error by Stephens overshadowed the fine play he made in the second inning when he leaped high in the air to snare a line drive from Cooper.

Marion popped up down the leftfield line and Laabs flagged it down in foul territory. Potter still had a chance to get out of the inning but he gave up a single to Verban which scored a run and one to pitcher Max Lanier to score another. Sewell came out to the mound and called on Muncrief to end the threat which he did.

The Browns were still down 3-1 in the sixth when they mounted a threat. Stephens grounded out to start things off but then Lanier got wild and walked Laabs and McQuinn. Both runners advanced on a wild pitch and that was all Southworth had to see. He summoned Ted Wilks who had lost the third game of the series.

Christman who had only two hits in the series grounded to Kurowski at third. Kurowski threw to the plate to get Laabs as McQuinn held at second. Hayworth then flied out and the inning was over.

There was nothing else the Browns could do. Wilks retired the side in order in the ninth, striking out Byrnes and Chartak after getting McQuinn on a foulout. The Cardinals jubilantly crowded around Wilks after winning their second series in three attempts.

The crowd stood and cheered the Cardinals for their victory and cheered the Browns for their fine season and tough play in the series.

If anything could be blamed for the Browns losing the series, it was their fielding. The team that finished third in the league in fielding committed ten errors, resulting in seven unearned runs. Two of the Browns' losses were due to errors at key points in the game. Because of the faulty fielding,

Chet Laabs scored the first run of the sixth game but that was all the Browns could do. (The Bettman Archive)

Galehouse would go 1-1 with a 1.50 earned run average and Potter and Muncrief would each have a loss, despite earned run averages of 0.93 and 1.35, respectively.

At the plate the Browns didn't fare much better as their .183 team batting average proved. After McQuinn's .438 average (the best on either team and excluding Mancuso's .667 with only three at bats) the second highest average on the team was Kreevich's .231. Stephens hit .227 and Laabs hit .200 leaving everyone else below the .200 mark.

Because of the war, World Series gate receipts totaled a little more than $900,000, lower than any amount during the Depression. Each Brownie got $2,744 which was the lowest total since 1920. Ten percent of that came in War Bonds.

The players joked for years after that Jakucki spent his share before leaving town.

When Bill DeWitt and Donald Barnes went to Cardinal owner Sam Beardon's office after the game to congratulate him, Beardon greeted them by saying, "If we'd have lost this series to the Browns, I'd have had to leave town. It would have been a disgrace to lose to the Browns." Already drowning in the disappointment of losing the series, DeWitt and Barnes managed to chuckle at the putdown.

Even after an exciting pennant race and making the Cardinals earn their World Series win, the Browns still couldn't get the respect they deserved.

AFTERWORD

"My sole reason for getting involved with the Browns was to rescue them from the doldrums with which they were always associated."

— Donald Barnes

On the second day of May the following season, the headlines of the St. Louis Post-Dispatch read: "WAR ENDS IN ITALY; NAZIS QUIT." The news overshadowed the raising of the only American League pennant in the Browns' history. On a chilly day with the threat of rain, the players were handed their rings. The ceremony was followed with the pennant flag being raised with the American flag. Only a little more than 12,000 came out to Sportsman's Park to witness the once in a lifetime occasion. The Browns would lose 2-1 in thirteen innings in a game that lasted three and a half hours (an eternity in that era).

The Browns got off to a slow start in '45 and finished in third place. It would be the last time the team finished over .500.

ONE CHAMPIONSHIP SEASON

Three months later Donald Barnes, the architect of a team with a future, stunned everyone by selling his stock in the team. Richard Muckerman who had held 25% of the team's stock purchased Barnes' 31%. Barnes left Muckerman and the Browns in the best financial shape they would ever find themselves in.

Muckerman retained Bill DeWitt (who was named Executive of the Year by *The Sporting News*) and Luke Sewell (who was named Manager of the Year by *The Sporting News*) with the promise that they had his full support. But whereas Sewell had a strong voice in the operation of the club under Barnes, he soon realized under Muckerman he was only field boss. Sewell was eventually fired after a 53-71 start in 1946. DeWitt and his brother Charley eventually purchased the team from Muckerman in 1949.

Muckerman was a lifetime Browns fan but chose to use the money the team had made for the remodeling of the park instead of the growth of the team on the field.

When the Browns signed one-armed Pete Gray in '45 it was with the understanding that his handicap would not be used for gate attraction. Sewell was to treat him like any other player but didn't. In 77 games Gray hit .218 and was platooned with Mike Kreevich who hit .300 for the American League Champions of the year before. Kreevich complained about the lack of playing time and was traded to the Senators. The dismissal of Kreevich signified the beginning of the end. Shortly afterward George Caster was sent to the eventual World Champion Tigers.

After the season, George McQuinn was traded to the Philadelphia A's for Dick Siebert. McQuinn's age was used as a reason but at 37 he was still a better player than Siebert (34) was in his prime. Siebert held out and never reported to the Browns.

The 1947 season turned out to be the season that tore apart the club. The team was in worse financial shape than they were during the Depression. Muckerman, with bills stacked on his desk and an empty ballpark, began selling off his best players. Before the season started he sold Chet Laabs to the Athletics. Within three days he had sent Bob Muncrief to the Indians for three players and $25,000 and Jack Kramer and Vern Stephens to Boston for six mediocre players and $310,000. When Denny Galehouse was sold to Boston during the winter, sportswriters began calling the Red Sox the Boston Browns. The fact that the Red Sox became a better team with many of those former Brownies suggests that it wasn't just the war years that won the pennant for St. Louis.

By the time the DeWitt brothers bought the team in January of 1949 only Al Zarilla remained from the pennant winning roster. Fifteen games into the '49 season he was traded.

After the DeWitt's failed to revive the dying franchise they sold the team to Bill Veeck in the summer of '51. Unfortunately, Veeck's desire to please the fans only made the Browns look more ridiculous in the fans' eyes, the worst evidence being Eddie Gaedel.

By the winter of 1953 major league owners were pushing Veeck into selling the ballclub. The consensus amongst all was to sell to interests in Los Angeles. Veeck, who didn't want to sell or move the team to California, finally sold the franchise to Baltimore brewing executive Jerry Hoffberger. Hoffberger renamed the team the Orioles.

Sportman's Park is gone now. It ceased to breath thirteen long years after the Browns left town. Augie Busch who by then owned the Cardinals, presented the deed to the ballpark to Richard Amberg who was the publisher of the *Globe-Democrat* and president of the Herbert Hoover Boys Club.

ONE CHAMPIONSHIP SEASON

A large playground, owned by the same Boys Club, now sits on the spot, so at least the real estate is still used for baseball as it has been since the Civil War era. A plaque sits where home plate used to be, immortalizing the plot of land forever. The old YMCA building and the billboard on a building roof to its left can still be seen.

But no longer do the 1944 American League Champion St. Louis Browns take the field and no longer do the streetcars line up on Grand Avenue awaiting the fans who departed the park after a hard fought game. But forever on that spot swirls the memories of one glorious championship season.

BIBLIOGRAPHY

Invaluable essays by David M. Jordan and Jim Donaghy were supplied by Len Levin of SABR and members of the St. Louis Browns Historical Society.

Other information in this book was culled from newpaper reports which were tracked almost day by day. The following writers work aided in the writing of this book: Edgar G. Brands, Harold C. Burr, Dan Daniel, Carl T. Felker, Ernest J. Lanigan, Frederick G. Lieb, Art Morrow, Shirley Povich, Paul A. Rickart, J.G. Taylor Spink & Joe Williams of the Sporting News; W.J. McGoogan and J. Roy Stockton of the St. Louis Post Dispatch & Hugh Fullerton Jr. of the Cape Girardeau Southeast Missourian.

The writings of James M. Gould in Baseball Magazine also attributed to the facts of the story.

The following books were invaluable in the author's research:

ADOMITES, PAUL. World of Baseball: October's Games. A Redefinition Book, 1990

ANDERSON, HARRY H. The Ancient Origins of Baseball In Milwaukee. Milwaukee History, Summer 1983, Vol. 6, Number 2, p.p. 42-57

BENSON, MICHAEL. Ballparks of North America: A Comprehensive Historical Reference to Baseball Grounds, Yards and Stadiums, 1845 to Present. McFarland & Company, Inc., Publishers, 1989

BORST, BILL (Editor) The Brown Stocking I. St. Louis Browns Historical Society, 1985 (written by members of the Society)

BORST, BILL. Baseball Through a Knothole: A St. Louis History. Krank Press, St. Louis, 1980

BORST, BILL & FISCHER, ERV. A Cornucopia of St. Louis Browns History and Trivia: A Jockstrap Full of Nails. St. Louis Browns Historical Society, 1992

BORST, BILL & JIM SCOTT (Editors) Ables to Zoldak: Vol. I, II & III. St. Louis Browns Fan Club, Krank Press, 1988 (written by members of the fan club)

BORST, BILL & WALDEN, GEORGE (Editors) The Brown Stocking II. St. Louis Browns Historical Society, 1987 (written by members of the Society)

CREAMER, ROBERT W. Baseball in '41. Penguin Books, 1991

FROMMER, HARVEY. Rickey & Robinson: The Men Who Broke Baseball's Color Line. MacMillan Publishing Co., Inc., N.Y. 1982

GILBERT, BILL They Also Served: Baseball And The Home Front, 1941-1945. Crown Publishers Inc., New York, 1992

GOWDY, CURT with POWERS, JOHN. Seasons to Remember: The Way It Was in American Sports 1945-1960. Harper Collins, N.Y., 1993

HALBERSTAM, DAVID. Summer of '49. William Morrow and Company, Inc., New York 1989

HILTON, GEORGE W. Milwaukee's Charter Membership In The A.L. Historical Messenger of the Milwaukee Historical Society, Spring 1974, p.p. 2-117

HONIG, DONALD. The American League: An Illustrated History. Crown Publishers, Inc., 1983

KAPLAN, JIM. The Fielders. A Redefinition Book, Virginia, 1989

Bibliography

MEAD, WILLIAM B. Baseball Goes to War: Stars Don Khaki, 4F's Vie For Pennant. (Originally published by Contemporary Books, Inc. under the title, Even The Browns, 1978) Farragut Publishing Co., 1985

MEAD, WILLIAM B. Two Spectacular Seasons. Macmillan Publishing Company, 1990

NEMEC, DAVID. The Great American Baseball Team Book. Penguin Books, N.Y., 1992

OKRENT, DANIEL & WULF, STEVE. Baseball Anecdotes. Oxford University Press, Inc., 1989

REIDENBAUGH, LOWELL. Take Me Out To The Ballgame. Revised Edition. Sports Illustrated Publishing Co., 1989

SEIDEL, MICHAEL. Streak: Joe DiMaggio and the Summer of '41. McGraw-Hill Book Company, 1988

SEYMOUR, HAROLD. Baseball: The Early Years. Oxford University Press, New York, 1960

SHATZKIN, MIKE (Editor) The Ballplayers. William Morrow & Company, 1990

SULLIVAN, NEIL J. The Minors. St. Martin's Press, N.Y. 1990

WILL, GEORGE F. Men at Work: The Craft of Baseball. Macmillan Publishing Company, 1990

ONE CHAMPIONSHIP SEASON

Index

Index